2—

RICOCHET

WHAT TO DO WHEN
CHANGE
HAPPENS TO YOU

RICOCHET

WHAT TO DO WHEN
CHANGE
HAPPENS TO YOU

NICK TASLER

BEAVER'S POND
PRESS

Edited by Wendy Weckwerth

ISBN 13: 978-1-59298-820-4
Library of Congress Catalog Number: 2017900935
Printed in the United States of America
First Printing: 2017
23 22 21 20 19   6 5 4 3 2

Cover design by Claire Chamberlin
Interior design by Athena Currier

 Beaver's Pond Press, Inc.
7108 Ohms Lane
Edina, MN 55439–2129

(952) 829-8818
www.BeaversPondPress.com

To order, visit www.ItascaBooks.com
or call 1-800-901-3480 ext. 118.
Reseller discounts available.

To Rueben, Franklin,
Lincoln, and Gwendolyn—
the four most unexpectedly delightful
ricochet events of my life.

CONTENTS

PART 1: FIND FREEDOM

PART 2: PURSUE PROGRESS

PART 3: MAKE MEANING

ACKNOWLEDGMENTS

AS MUCH AS I'D LIKE TO BELIEVE that this book is exclusively the result of my innate brilliance, that belief would be approximately one hundred eighty degrees away from the truth. I need to start by acknowledging Scott and Abby Siepmann, Josh and Stephanie Masters, Adam and McKenzi King, Tony Gargano, Nate and Brooke Odem, Nick Wernimont, Jeff Cantalupo, and John and Julie Gaffey. Years ago, their investment of money and confidence ensured that the strategies, stories, and inspiration in this book would reach your eyes and ears instead of collecting mental mildew somewhere in the crevices of my brain. Their trust and loyalty humbles me on a daily basis. If you're ever lucky enough to cross their paths, give them a thank-you—and to really up the awkwardness ante—make sure to also give them a hug.

I also want to thank Cliff Allen for continuing to go way beyond the call of duty when it comes to keeping my professional affairs in order during my frequent excursions through la-la land; and my wife Alison for doing pretty much the exact same thing on the home front. Thanks to Wendy Weckwerth and Lily Coyle for shaping up this manuscript and reminding me not to overlook the basic essentials of bookmaking. The collective wisdom of Jeff Prouty, John Stout, Kevin Wilde, Steve Cohen, and Karen Grabow is reflected somewhere somehow on every page of this book. The team at BrightSight Group deserve credit for fine-tuning the idea and keeping me in touch with my audience.

Lastly, this book would literally not be the same without the highly resilient and heroic strangers, clients, friends, and family members who so generously shared their stories and hard-won wisdom with me. Some are mentioned by name, and many more are not—but I'm immensely grateful for them all.

INTRODUCTION

●

CALIFORNIA DREAMIN'
MEETS ICE, ICE, AND A BABY

A WHILE BACK, THE UNIVERSE took a running start and drop-kicked me in the crotch.

The year was 2007. I was a small-town boy from Iowa who had spent the previous four years living the dream on the sun-drenched beaches of southern California. Shortly after arriving in San Diego, I met a smart, pretty, and fun girl named Alison. After a whirlwind nine-month romance, I impulsively asked her to marry me. Even though my proposal came sans engagement ring, she impulsively said yes. After I finished graduate school in the summer of 2005, Alison and I got married, and then spent two months backpacking through Europe.

For the rest of 2005 and 2006, the dream sequence continued. I had taken a position as the director of new-product development at the psychological research and consulting company, TalentSmart. After doing mostly technology and process consulting at Accenture for the first few years of my career, I was finally doing the kind of work I was utterly fascinated with and obnoxiously passionate about. Over lunch breaks I went surfing with my boss, Travis, who had also become a good friend. When I drove home to our cozy apartment on the bluffs of Del Mar after work every night, I was greeted with a truly breathtaking panoramic view of the Pacific Ocean. On more than one occasion, I literally pinched myself.

And then 2007 happened.

In January of that year, my fifty-six-year-old father had a massive heart attack and was technically dead for almost a minute before being revived. Two days later, he miraculously survived an emergency five-bypass surgery. A month later Alison and I packed up our Del Mar apartment into a little U-Haul trailer, said good-bye to our San Diego friends, and backed out of the driveway for the last time.

Then we received an omen.

After waving good-bye to our friends, my seven-months-pregnant wife and I started driving up that big hill. The same huge hill that provided those gorgeous, pinch-inspiring panoramic views of the ocean when you're driving downhill lost much of its charm when you had to drive uphill. We had gone approximately twenty yards before the tires on our four-cylinder Nissan Sentra started spinning out, and we ground to a halt.

Our friends had a good laugh. I made some quip about how this must be San Diego's way of giving us one more chance to rethink our decision to move back to the upper Midwest. On the outside, I was laughing. On the inside, I was seriously contemplating this supernatural possibility. Right about then is when it also occurred to me that this hill was just the beginning. In order to get to the Midwest, we still had to cross a little strip of slightly uneven terrain called the Rocky Mountains. In February.

Nonetheless, I backed down the hill to where it flattened out a bit so I could build up some momentum. Then I took a deep breath and gunned it. We got up the hill, and we even made it through the Rockies. Two weeks and a three-day snowstorm delay later, we pulled up to my wife's parents' house in a small town in southern Minnesota.

We had made it.

Sort of.

Thus began the single worst year of our marriage, and arguably the worst year of my life.

We spent the next three months living with my in-laws while we hunted for a house to buy. Although I have since come to love my in-laws' house and that little town where my wife grew up, at that time in my life, it was my Siberia.

In mid-May, our first son, Rueben, was born. Two weeks later, we moved out of my in-laws' and into a house we bought in Minneapolis. Once there, things only got worse. Much worse.

When I took stock of the situation in my head—as I did multiple times every day (maladaptive habit number one)—my recap looked like this:

I had gone from having two fully functioning parents to having a nearly dead dad.

I had replaced sandy beaches with icy streets.

I had traded daily surfing sessions for endless home repairs on an eighty-year-old house with lots of "character" two thousand miles from the nearest ocean.

I used to sleep soundly and now was being awakened every hour by a wailing infant.

I used to have lots of friends to hang out with, and now I had almost none.

I used to have super-fun coworkers. Now I spent each day conversing with a carved wooden duck.

The relaxed and romantic dinners I had enjoyed with my bride were permanently infiltrated by a screaming parasite with stinky diapers.

Alison and I used to exchange warm gazes as we passed words of praise to one another. Now we exchanged icy glares as we handed off parental to-do lists and home-repair status updates.

We used to be fun-loving newlyweds who traveled the world. Now we were depressed new parents who never left the house.

One day I was in the driver's seat. The next day I was strapped to the hood of a '74 Pinto.

The most soul-crushing part was it felt like this was simply how my life was going to be from now on. I started to think maybe this is just what "real life" looked like on the other side of the honeymoon. Miserable. Permanently.

My life has been a living hell ever since.

Just kidding.

The misery wasn't permanent. We got through it. I can't say exactly when it happened, but sometime a year or two later, it just occurred to me: *we're good now*. I didn't know exactly why. It's not like big changes had stopped coming—not by a long shot. But evidently something had changed about the way we were handling the changes. We had somehow stumbled onto an adaptation strategy that worked.

And now—nine years, four houses, two apartments, one duplex, three more kids, three different states, two seismic career shifts, one financial crisis, and a move to Puerto Rico later—my wife and I are closer than ever. My kids no longer suck my will to live and I even kind of, sort of, love hanging out with them more than anything else in the world.

But do you know the best thing of all?

We've stopped fearing change.

It's not that we started believing every change is positive. Let's be real. Some changes stink. Coating those turds with sugar won't make them doughnuts. But now we know we can adapt to everything from marital troubles, family issues, financial problems, and job changes to natural disasters, language barriers, new cities, new states, new climates, and new geographies. And when you finally realize you can adapt to whatever life throws at you, a magical thing happens.

You no longer feel compelled to control the future. You feel liberated to explore it.

Upon realizing this, most normal human beings probably would have breathed a sigh of relief, counted their blessings, and moved on with their lives. But I couldn't let it go. I became obsessed with figuring out just what exactly was enabling us to adapt. What were we doing, thinking, feeling, and saying that was working for us? But also, where were we still screwing up?

I thought if I could find clear answers to those questions, then maybe I could replicate our strategy. And if *we* could replicate it, then so could my friends and my family and my clients. They could free themselves from the fear of changes in their work, in their relationships, in their kids, in their health, and in their finances. They could finally be free to explore a whole new world of possibilities right under their noses.

That, my friend, is why you're reading this book.

To solve the puzzle of adaptation, I began digging through troves of scientific studies; interviewing hundreds of real people experiencing significant change; quizzing dozens of researchers and practitioners with the relentless fervor of a caffeinated kindergartner on a field trip to the zoo; and then stacking up all that data against my own experiences. Along the way, I discovered a heaping pile of half-truths, universal misconceptions, and surprising secrets about adaptation. Such as the importance of thinking positive (sort of true and sort of not); surrounding yourself with friends (depends *which* friends); talking more openly about your feelings (huge caveat on this warm and fuzzy fave); the importance of reducing stress (fatally misguided); and the time-honored American pursuit of happiness (kind of sad, actually). I also discovered why inspiration is more likely on Tuesdays than Fridays; why bad luck inspires creative superpowers; what true freedom looks like in real life; and why adaptation to change is actually much simpler than we've been led to believe.

When the dust settled and my head cleared, three basic factors stood out:

1. Find freedom.
2. Pursue progress.
3. Make meaning.

As much as I really wanted to include a fourth factor—appreciate alliteration—the evidence just didn't support its adaptive value. (Not that I love it any less as a literary device.)

The rest of this book is going to show you how to apply those three factors to navigating whatever change you're going through right now, and then to set you free to start living the adventurous life you've always secretly dreamed about.

PART 1

FIND FREEDOM

1

●

WHAT HAPPENED WHEN MA GOT HER BELL RUNG

ANDY AND CHUCK WERE LEADING similar lives when the fog fell.

Andy was a snappy-dressing, middle-aged man with well-groomed hair, polished shoes, and a pleasing personality. Chuck was a lot like Andy, except he was a few years older and a little smaller in stature. Each lived on a tree-lined street in a cozy Chicago suburb with their devoted wives and healthy kids. As their children had grown, so had Andy's and Chuck's careers at the phone company. Both men had shimmied their way up the company totem pole until they reached comfortable slots in the ranks of management.

The way most of their friends and family members saw it, Chuck and Andy had it made. For almost the entire twentieth century, a job at the phone company guaranteed great benefits and lifetime employment. But as the bright-green leaves began turning brown and crunchy in the autumn of 1981, Andy's and Chuck's jobs seemed to follow suit.

It had been a hundred years since the famed inventor Alexander Graham Bell had created the phone company later commonly known as Ma Bell. During that century, Ma Bell enjoyed complete dominion over the sprawling web of telephone lines running from Ellis Island to Hollywood and connecting the northern shores of Lake Superior to the southern tips of Texas and the Gulf shores of Florida. To dial up Ma Bell's pre-Internet communication web, all average Americans had to do was pick up the phone—a piece of hardware they also had to buy from Ma Bell.

Everything was swell for Andy and Chuck and their families right up until Ma started showing her age. In the 1960s and 1970s, the phone lines started going down more and more often. Calls were getting dropped with increasing regularity. And as comedian Lily Tomlin illustrated with her wildly popular *Laugh-In* skit—the only thing worse than the phone service at Ma Bell was the customer service at Ma Bell.

So what could Ma Bell's long-suffering customers do with their boiling exasperation?

Not a thing. If you didn't like Ma Bell, your only other communication options were the Pony Express, carrier pigeons, or two cans and a string.

As more and more Americans started sporting bell-bottoms, Ma Bell started looking more and more like a monopoly. And Americans in the 1970s hated big corporate monopolies almost as much as they hated the Vietnam War and fuel-efficient cars. Chuck, Andy, and the rest of America had known it was only a matter of time before the U.S. government forced Ma Bell to kick her so-called Baby Bells out of the nest.

Although everybody believed that the shake-up would give everyday Americans a cheaper and more reliable way to call their moms, make dentist appointments, and catch up with old friends on the other side of the country, nobody was optimistic about how this massive change would impact the hundreds of thousands of phone company employees like Chuck and Andy, and their families.

Just like amputating an infected leg—knowing it needs to happen doesn't change the fact that it's going to hurt.

Once people had worked their way up to a manager's title at the phone company, everyone just assumed those managers would stay there until the day they collected their gold watches and their first pension check. And why wouldn't they assume that? That is exactly what had happened to hundreds of thousands of phone company employees for nearly a century.

But now the future seemed uncertain at best and downright nightmarish at worst. Chuck and Andy found themselves looking over the edge of one of the most momentous shifts in American industry since the breakup of J. D. Rockefeller's Standard Oil Company. And nobody could see the bottom.

Finally, in 1981, the fog hanging over Andy's and Chuck's jobs took a viscous turn—from pea soup to clam chowder.

In a matter of months, half of Chuck's and Andy's twenty-six thousand coworkers in the Illinois Bell offices were pushed out the door of the only company they had ever worked for. The result was bedlam. Heart attacks. Divorces. Strokes. Cancers. Suicides. Kidney failures. Drug abuse. Rampant alcoholism. Gambling addictions. Every other stress-related malady you could imagine infected Andy's and Chuck's friends and teammates. Illinois Bell was a full-blown disaster area littered with the physical and psychological wreckage of its workforce.

Andy panicked.

Even though he was one of the lucky ones who didn't lose his job, he started to lose his mind. Before

Ma Bell plunged him into the fog, Andy saw himself as a vital "link in the chain of command." He showed up to work; gave his bosses a pleasing smile and a firm handshake; collected his marching orders for the day; regurgitated those orders to his underlings; and was home by dinner.

Now, everything was different. On this strange new playing field, none of his bosses had ever thrown a ball or swung at a pitch. They were just as befuddled as he was. They could no longer give him orders, even if they'd wanted to.

Even when he left the office at night, Andy could think of nothing but the horrors of his unruly work environment. A nasty cycle developed in which Andy would come home to his wife who would kindly and compassionately ask him to share his feelings about what was going on. Andy's sharing would escalate to venting, which erupted into insults, which wounded the one person who was trying hardest to comfort him. Andy would calm down, and then feel guilty about lashing out. A few days later, the cycle would start all over again. His blood pressure shot up. He developed an ulcer. Andy was falling apart, inside and out.

What about Chuck?

For Chuck, the timing could not have been worse. When the hammer fell on the phone company, his fifty-something age trapped him in a vocational no-man's-land—too young to retire, but too old to find another job. Both of his teenaged kids would soon be entering college, and his wife had dreams of going back to finish the college degree she'd long ago abandoned for motherhood.

An engineer by training, Chuck had slid over to customer relations years before, which meant his job duties wouldn't allow him to hide behind the phone company's Byzantine bureaucracy. Each and every day Chuck had to report for duty at the front line of the battle and deal with the endless onslaught of angry callers.

And yet, Chuck didn't come unglued.

Despite a heart that was years older than Andy's, his blood pressure didn't spike. Despite the sudden and forceful disruption of three decades of work habits, Chuck didn't develop an ulcer. He didn't fight more often with his wife. He didn't ignore his kids. He didn't spend more time betting on horses at the track or bellying up to the bar at the pub.

While immersed in the fog of confusion and uncertainty, Chuck did what puzzled, scared, frustrated, and hurting human beings have done for thousands of years in the wake of all sorts of unexpected changes. He did what housewives have done when they find out the truth about their cheating husbands; what apparently healthy adults have done when a doctor delivers a disturbing diagnosis; what teenaged parents have done when they see the little blue line on a pregnancy test; what families who had built a perfect life in one neighborhood do when a job transfer sends them to strange lands; what millions of everyday people did when the stock market crashed in 1929 and the housing bubble burst in 2008; what tens of thousands of European Jews did when they walked out the gates of Auschwitz alone and traumatized; what ravaged parents did after leaving the cemetery without their child. Chuck did what one out of three people have always done in the wake of the endless, inexplicable twists of fate known to our species.

He adapted.

THE SECRET OF THE ADAPTIVE THIRD

Chuck and Andy faced the same change at the same place in the same year with the same stakes on the line.

Chuck found inspiration. Andy found imprisonment.

Why? How did Chuck do it? Why didn't Andy do the same thing?

Fortunately for us, a clever psychologist named Salvatore R. Maddi and a curious executive named Carl Horn had the foresight to ask these questions six years before the breakup of Ma Bell. The result is one of the most fascinating field experiments ever conducted on human adaptability.

It all began in 1974 when Maddi made a startling discovery. Not from one of his own studies, but from other research cited by an article in *Family Circle* magazine. The article explained how important it was to avoid stressful circumstances, because they will kill us. And the best way to avoid stressful circumstances, the article argued, was to avoid changing circumstances.

But Maddi's research was showing something very different than those other studies in the *Family Circle*. He was studying creative people and finding over and over again that creative people do not avoid changes. In fact, they seemed to prefer them. They somehow intuitively knew that fluctuating situations are more likely to inspire flashes of creative genius. And yet the *Family Circle* article implied that anyone who is crazy enough to seek out changing circumstances must have a death wish.

That just didn't make sense to Maddi. He thought there must be something different about the way the people in his studies handled change versus the way the folks in the *Family Circle* article were handling change. That gave him an idea.

Maddi had already become friends with Carl Horn while doing psychological consulting work at the phone company. So he reached out to Horn and asked him what he thought about the idea of Maddi and his team studying Illinois Bell's employees before, during, and after the breakup. Horn loved the idea.

For the next twelve years Maddi and his team of researchers at the University of Chicago used Illinois Bell as their laboratory. They followed hundreds of people and monitored everything you could imagine. They were right there taking notes, asking questions, and reading blood pressures as coworkers moved from one cubicle to the next; as one boss left and a new one started; as the American economy inched up and slid back down again; as new kids were born and older kids switched schools; as marriages changed and mortgages were paid; as Jimmy Carter took over from Gerald Ford, and when Carter handed the reigns to Ronald Reagan.

When the breakup finally happened, six years into his study, half the people in the study were laid off by Ma Bell while the other half stayed on. Maddi and his team continued to keep tabs on both groups for the next six years. What they found was intriguing.

The majority of people—whether they kept their jobs or lost their jobs—shared Andy's experience. The sudden change brought them to their knees.

But a third of the people in both groups didn't just survive. They thrived.

Those in the adaptive third didn't have heart attacks or marital troubles or gambling addictions. Those who stayed on at Illinois Bell became high-ranking leaders in the dramatically altered organization. Those who were laid off became rising stars at their new companies.

Most surprising of all was how very *ordinary* the people in the adaptive third were. On paper, they looked just like everyone else. Maddi and Horn's analysis showed they weren't more adaptive because they experienced fewer stressful experiences. They weren't more adaptive because they had better bosses. They weren't more adaptive because they had happier home lives. They weren't more educated. They weren't smarter. They didn't have fancier titles or easier jobs. They didn't have privileged childhoods. And they weren't born with special genetic gifts.

What separated the adaptive third from everyone else is surprisingly simple: while the others were busy trying to bounce back, the adaptive third took small steps forward.

THE BOUNCE-BACK MYTH

A ricochet event is any unexpected or unwelcome change that knocks us off course. When a ricochet event happens, every normal functioning human brain is wired to ask the same question: *What does this mean?* Our minds launch a full-scale search for answers to resolve our confusion.

But we don't all look in the same place.

When Andy and most of his coworkers looked around and saw nothing but thick fog in every direction, they did what most of us instinctively do when we get lost. They retraced their steps.

Before the change happened, Andy told Maddi's researchers, "I know each day what I have to do and how to do it." He liked it that way. So when the disruptions began, Andy recoiled. In Maddi and Deborah M. Khoshaba's excellent training guide *Resilience at Work*, he explains that Andy was consumed with how things used to be in the "good ol' days of more precise company objectives and plans."

When Maddi's team asked Andy about his plans for the future, he replied with anxious mumbles and shifty stares. When he finally sputtered out a reply, his image of the future looked suspiciously similar to the past. He wanted his work to be predictable again. He wanted to know what to expect again. He wanted to be able to prove to his bosses that he was still a crucial link in an unbreakable chain of command. He wanted to go back to a time and place where he could go home at night to his wife and kids, knowing exactly what he would find when he showed up at work the next day. He wanted to bounce back to a place that no longer existed.

When the fog settled over Chuck, he didn't try to bounce back.

Just like Andy, Chuck's brain also went searching for answers. He also asked himself *what does this mean?* But while Andy was busy trying to make sense of what he *had done* to deserve this plunge into the fog, Chuck tried to make sense of what he *could do* now that he had been plunged into the fog.

When Chuck's brain returned from its scouting mission, it brought back a brilliantly simple idea for trying to find out what his customers really wanted from their phone service, and then comparing it to what Illinois Bell had been offering them.

Most of Chuck's bosses, as well as his peers like Andy, missed such obvious solutions because they were consumed with trying to figure out how they had fallen into this fog-draped pit of angst.

Meanwhile Chuck was taking one small step at a time in the opposite direction, moving forward instead of looking backward. Chuck went on to enjoy six more years of exciting work before retiring from the new and improved company he helped create.

THE RIGHT QUESTION

As the Illinois Bell melee was unfolding, a young graduate student named Roxane Cohen Silver was just up the shore of Lake Michigan at Northwestern University studying how ordinary people cope with loss and trauma. Silver discovered that two out of three grieving widows, bereaved parents, and victims of terrorism, child abuse, and natural disasters instinctively look for meaning in the past. They try to find some explanation for their suffering.

For years and years, nearly all psychologists assumed that was a universal reaction in the wake of traumatic change, and that therefore, adapting to change and adversity requires finding an explanation.

But they were wrong.

In study after study over the past three decades, Silver and her colleagues have found that a remarkably consistent one out of three trauma victims will *not* search for a reason to explain why they are experiencing misfortune. And they turn out to be the most well-adjusted—weeks, months, and years later.

Silver has found an adaptive third among elderly widows who had woken up next to their husbands every day for decades until the day when they had to start waking up to the eerie silence of an empty house.

She has found an adaptive third among moms and dads who have suffered the unspeakable agony of throwing dirt on the casket of their little boy or girl.

She has identified an adaptive third among innocent kids whose number-one wish before blowing out their birthday candles every year was that Mommy and Daddy would start protecting them instead of smacking or fondling them.

She has also found an adaptive third among people who watched wildfires turn their dream homes into piles of smoldering ash.

Roxane Cohen Silver's and Salvatore Maddi's research both point to the same conclusion. When change happens, two out of three people will spend months, years, and even lifetimes going back to the scene of the crime in search of some explanation for their woes. Sadly, the only thing most of them will ever find is more suffering.

But they don't have to.

One-third of these bereaved widows, grieving parents, disoriented professionals, corporate managers, forest-fire victims, and child-abuse survivors will do something different. They will take one small step forward and then another and another and another. These people will end up more confident, more content, more fulfilled, and more successful weeks, months, and years later.

That is the first and most important lesson of *Ricochet*: Instead of asking why bad things happen to good people, adaptive people turn that timeless riddle on its head and ask what can good people do when bad things happen?

2

●

SARAH AND THE EXPLORER

You are free, and that is why you are lost.

—Franz Kafka

IT WAS A LITTLE AFTER NINE O'CLOCK and Sarah J. Smith still had a stack of student papers to review. She sat in a pair of yoga pants and a baggy sweatshirt with her hair pulled back and her legs casually folded under the old wooden desk on which her grandmother had long ago signed checks and written letters. On the streets below her apartment, downtown Toronto buzzed with the urban symphony of accelerating engines, squeaky brakes, and the chatter of pedestrians in pursuit of the next heated destination.

But fourteen floors above the street noise, there were only the sounds of Sarah's breath and the occasional ripple of a turning page or scribble of a note in the margin. Sarah's gaze had wandered out the window, over the tiny balcony, and out into the black winter night.

Suddenly, an idea popped into her head. *Someday, you will fund microloans to women in impoverished nations.*

"It was so clear I thought I might have overheard a conversation," she told me. But there was nobody around. Her husband Michael wasn't home. No one was chatting outside her apartment door.

"I honestly knew nothing about microloans. This was 1997," she explained. "Muhammad Yunus hadn't yet won the Nobel Peace Prize [for microlending in Bangladesh]. Micro entrepreneurship wasn't in the headline news."

Even though today billions of dollars are loaned and repaid through this innovative practice in which ordinary people volunteer to make personal loans of as little as twenty-five dollars to help farmers, craftsmen, and merchants in poorer parts of the world get their businesses up and running, microlending wasn't widely talked about back in the 1990s.

Crazy as it was, Sarah's idea stuck with her. "The thought was so crystal clear. I couldn't get it out of my mind."

She stayed up most of the night thinking about it, and continued thinking about in the weeks that followed. Over the next few years, a series of odd coincidences and unlikely meetings sent Sarah on a wild journey crisscrossing the globe from Canada to China to Central America and back to her hometown in western Wisconsin. The result was Sarah's Hope Jewelry.

Sarah's first product, a piece called Elia Rose, was a magnificent sparkling blue and green pendant shaped like a tortilla in honor of its namesake. Elia Rose, the woman, was a single mother from Nicaragua who supported her family by making and selling tortillas to her neighbors. With a microloan from Sarah's Hope and its customers, Elia Rose could finally afford to buy flour in bulk, which increased her tortilla profits just enough to comfortably send her kids to school and buy them the medicine they needed.

When I met Smith in 2010, Sarah's Hope had already been named among the top fifteen hottest-selling brands in the jewelry industry for the previous two years. It remained a fixture on the list for another five years. In that time, Sarah's Hope has empowered thousands of impoverished single moms and struggling female entrepreneurs like Elia Rose to create successful businesses that can support their families and turn the tide of generational poverty.

Nobody is more surprised about the success of Sarah's Hope than Sarah Smith.

She is fit and pretty and looks a decade younger than she is. With her long and thick reddish-brown hair, she can pull off elegance whenever the jewelry industry requires it. Yet, she still can't help releasing a screechy giggle when she considers how unlikely it is that *she* is the founder of a successful jewelry business. Before she started Sarah's Hope, she claims she "didn't even hardly wear jewelry. Plus," she says with a cocked eyebrow and a grin, "I would have assumed one had to be able to draw—to *design*—if one were to own such a business."

At her core, Smith is a tomboy who is just as comfortable fixing fences on her family's cattle farm as she is displaying her latest designs at glitzy tradeshows for jewelry-store owners. If you paid her a visit today, it's likely that the only accessory you'd see sparkling in the light is the trusty pair of steel vice grips she hangs from her belt in a leather holster.

And yet, here she is. The path she took to get here gives us an important clue about how our brains respond to a ricochet event.

THE KAFKA EFFECT

Sarah Smith's journey began a few weeks before that strange night in her Toronto apartment. She and her husband, Michael, had just moved to Canada from New Jersey where she had completed a master's degree at Princeton University. Despite her dyslexia, Smith had always been a good student with a strong work ethic and a magnetic personality. She had been married for ten years to a man she loved. She was traveling down a career path she was passionate about. Although still getting used to life in a high-rise apartment in the heart of a city, the small-town girl saw the challenging adjustment as a necessary part of an exciting journey. Graduate school would be finished in a few years, and she saw visions of babies on the horizon.

Life was good. Which is probably why she didn't notice the signs.

There was a scheduling mix-up here. Some suspicious phone calls there. There were also Michael's subtle foot-dragging about children, and a few isolated incidents of finger-pointing and flying accusations from acquaintances.

But Sarah didn't put all those pieces together until she accidentally discovered the damning evidence on their computer. Only then did Michael finally tell her the truth about the secret affairs he'd been having. Although Michael insisted they try counseling, he slipped up again a few months later, and this time they both knew it was over.

"I was devastated," she told me.

For the first time in her life she suddenly found herself completely alone thousands of miles from home. The one person she had been able to count on to stay by her side and support her everywhere she'd been for the past ten years was now gone—and her clear understanding of the way life was supposed to unfold left with him. The fact that Michael was having affairs with men, instead of women, only intensified her confusion. Two false-positive HIV tests exacerbated her fear and anxiety.

Sarah's GPS had abruptly lost its signal.

Logically, she knew marriages fall apart all the time for any number of reasons. But she never expected that *her* marriage would end, and certainly not under circumstances of infidelity. She was haunted by questions that didn't seem to have answers. *Why did this happen? Why hadn't I seen it coming? What am I supposed to do now?*

Some people might label Sarah's situation "Kafkaesque"—a term used to describe situations that resemble the bizarre plots and strange events in the stories created by the early twentieth-century writer Franz Kafka.

A few years ago, a pair of psychologists named Travis Proulx and Steven J. Heine wanted to find out what happens inside our minds when we find ourselves in these Kafkaesque situations. So the researchers brought two groups of participants into Heine's laboratory at the University of British Columbia, and asked each group to read a different version of a Kafka story. Here's an excerpt from *The Country Doctor* the first group read:

> The youngster heaved himself up from under the feather bedding, threw his arms around my neck, and whispered in my ear, "Pull my tooth." I glanced around the room. No one had heard it. The parents were leaning forward in silence waiting for my verdict.
>
> I yielded, and leaned my head to the boy's face, which shivered under my wet beard. I confirmed what I already knew; the boy had no teeth.
>
> But as I shut my bag and put an arm out for my fur coat, the mother, apparently disappointed in me—why, what did these people expect?—biting her lips with tears in her eyes, the sister fluttering a towel, I was somehow ready to admit conditionally that the boy might have teeth after all.
>
> I went toward him, he welcomed me smiling, as if I were bringing him a delicious candy—and this time I discovered that the boy did indeed have teeth. In his right molar, near the back, was an

open cavity, dark brown, in many varia-
tions of shade.

But on a closer inspection there
was another complication. Worms were
wriggling from their fastness in the interior of the cavity toward the light, with
small white heads and many little legs.

Are you confused? Maybe disgusted? If so, that's the point.

The story continues on for another twenty or so
pages—each one chock full of absurd plot twists that
make absolutely no sense. At one point, the dentist's
neighbor inexplicably gets down on his hands and knees
and acts like a horse while wooing away the dentist's pretty
young love interest. All the while, the dentist feels much
like Sarah Smith did. He knows how absurd these events
are, but he can't explain them and he can't ignore them.

The second group of people in the British Columbia
study read a different version. It was the same basic story,
except this story made sense. One event led to another
the way you would expect. The little boy with a toothache
actually has teeth, and none of those teeth were spawning
worms. A friendly neighbor volunteered his horse, but he
didn't proceed to act like one. You get the picture.

Now, here's the fascinating part.

Shortly after study participants read the stories,
the researchers assigned each group to a task. The people

in each group were told to spot hidden patterns in random rows of letters. When the researchers tallied the results, they discovered that something strange had happened. The people who read the absurd Kafka story were able to correctly spot *twice as many* hidden patterns as the group who read the normal story.

Let that sink in for a moment.

The only difference between the two groups was that one of them read a confusing story. The other one read a coherent story. But for some odd reason the people who read the nonsensical story seemed to act twice as smart.

Since then, the British Columbia researchers have found the same bizarre results in study after study. After analyzing incoherent word pairs that have nothing to do with each other, such as "turn–frogs," "careful–sweaters," and "quickly–blueberries," a different group of people also spotted more patterns in random rows of letters than did a group of other people who read words they expected to see paired together, such as "hot–lava" and "cheese–cake."

The same thing happened after one group of people watched an inscrutable short film in which an ordinary family—mom, dad, brother Tommy, and sister Suzie—sit around an ordinary dinner table in an ordinary dining room eating an ordinary dinner . . . while wearing full-body rabbit costumes.

Huh? Exactly. The people who watched that strange clip for a few minutes spotted more correct patterns than people who watched a coherent clip from *The Simpsons*. (Homer might be ridiculous, but apparently there is sound logic to his ridiculousness.)

What's going on here? Why does ingesting nonsense make us smarter?

THE EXPLORER

It turns out that inside each of our minds lives a small but mighty explorer. The explorer spends our days scanning the environment for things that make us go *hmmm*. Most days we wake up, we eat breakfast, we go to work, we come home, we eat dinner, and we go to bed. Nothing unusual or unexpected happens, and so our explorers stay holed up like a Rocky Mountain survivalist in a region right behind our temples near a part of our brain called the anterior cingulate cortex.

But when something unexpected happens—like the neighbor in the Kafka story acts like a horse for no reason, or your spouse starts acting like a horse's hindquarters, or the boss who told you how valuable you are suddenly hands you a pink slip—your explorer leaps into action. It unleashes a psychological superpower designed to do one thing extremely well: find meaning.

It's as if a sudden change acts like a bat signal projected into the night sky. Once the explorer spots the signal, she puts on her cape and flies off to go make sense of the world again. It's like the hundred-pound mom who lifts the car to save her baby, except in this case the strength is mental rather than physical.

The problem is that some confusing events have no explanation. Meriwether Lewis and William Clark were great explorers. But they never found a waterway to the Pacific Ocean. Why? Because there isn't one.

So what does your explorer do when she (or he) can't explain why your partner is suddenly being a jerk or why Neighbor Brown is wearing a saddle and licking a salt block? What does the explorer do when year after year of stellar performance reviews culminates with a layoff?

She compensates. She tries to find meaning in another area to fill the void. That's when the magic happens.

Your explorer begins hunting for unrelated connections between ideas and objects that were probably right in front of us all along, but we just never noticed before. She might spot patterns in random strings of letters. Or bust through writer's block. Or unleash a burst of colorful creativity. She might even reveal our purpose in life.

Sarah Smith's epiphany offers a perfect example of the Kafka Effect. Something about her strange new surroundings in downtown Toronto and the barely noticeable, unexplained changes in her husband's behavior caught the attention of her explorer. While her conscious brain was busy thinking about the daily tasks of school and work, her explorer was scouring the landscape for a way forward.

To find the scent, her explorer paid a visit to her hippocampus—the brain's memory hub—where she sifted through images of important thoughts and events from Sarah's relevant past. Since Sarah ran a small sales and marketing business to put herself through theology school, her explorer kept bumping into the themes of business, faith, and social justice. So the explorer tucked those themes into her knapsack and kept hunting.

Maybe confusion about her marriage creeping into her consciousness inspired the "empowering women" motif, or maybe it was a core value that had always been there and was now being reactivated. Either way, the explorer stuffed that idea in her knapsack too. Eventually, the explorer stumbled onto a forgotten news article about microfinance, or a glanced-at flyer on the school's bulletin board, and . . . *aha!*

Someday, you will fund microloans to women in impoverished nations.

SEED INCIDENTS

In her studies of creative writers, psychologist Charlotte L. Doyle found that witnessing a curious encounter at a coffee shop or experiencing an emotionally charged event on the freeway can plant the seed for a new story—or plot twist or new character. She calls this a "seed incident." Seed incidents are often the first step in the creative process.

Because of your explorer, a ricochet event can become a seed incident.

For Sarah Smith, the seed incident was a disrupted marriage that inspired a new purpose for her life.

For busy professionals, the seed incident could be a job loss that spawns an idea for a successful new business, an exciting new career path, or a new set of priorities that moves the people in your life above the goals for your career.

A shake-up at work can become the seed incident for discovering something as simple as a new persona. After a frightening and frustrating three-year wave of lay-offs and departmental shuffling at Tim Peterson's Fortune 500 employer, Peterson had an epiphany.

"I remember coming out of this team meeting where the negativity was worse than ever," Peterson told me. "I walked out of this little conference room with these seven other people and as I was silently judging them for being so negative, I thought 'what are *you* doing?' You're not any better!

"But then it occurred to me that these new people on my team don't know me. They don't know anything about what I'm like, so I can choose to be whoever I want to be. I'd always been pretty timid before, and that's what people expected from me. I was the nice guy who just went along with the group. But then I decided to become the 'bold guy.' People were getting laid off left and right, regardless of what they said or did. So why not? I'm still not a jerk or anything. But now people look to me for answers and opinions in a way that didn't happen that much before. It's pretty cool."

For me, my dad's heart attack coupled with the stressful move from California to Minnesota was the seed incident that inspired my first book. I'd been chipping away at this idea for over a year with little bouts of progress here and there, but nothing substantial. I'd also been able to get a few agents to look at my idea, mostly as favors to mutual friends. But none of them wanted to represent me or the book.

Then on the tumultuous drive from San Diego to Minneapolis, in the midst of battling snowstorms and lugging a U-Haul trailer through the Rockies behind a compact car with a very pregnant and very nauseated wife, the right idea for the book suddenly and almost magically popped into my head. Just a little over a month later, after we pulled into my in-laws' driveway, I'd finished the forty-page book proposal, found a literary agent, and had three major publishers engaged in a bidding war before Simon & Schuster made an offer I couldn't refuse.

Given what I now know about publishing, I'm even more amazed about that turn of events today than I was then. If I hadn't lived it, I wouldn't believe it.

I didn't realize until years later that the inspiration that led to the accomplishment of this lifelong dream didn't happen in spite of the chaos surrounding me. It happened because of it.

Unfortunately, I was still too miserable in every other aspect of my life to enjoy this once-in-a-lifetime achievement. In fact, I was so busy wallowing in self-pity that I almost resented the book deal. In my mind, this outlandish dream that had actually come true was just one more obligation, one more nail in the coffin of my formerly carefree lifestyle. Pathetic, I know.

The point is that ricochet events—even events of the intensely sucky variety—will activate your explorer in a way that happy and stable times rarely do. No matter how torturous or baffling the change, your highly skilled explorer is now on the hunt. It's often right there in that messy, scary period of search and discovery that many of our most important innovations, our legacy-leaving creations, begin taking shape.

Nobody knew this truth better than the lawyer by day and writer by night, Franz Kafka. During the final months of 1912—one of his darkest periods, which was anchored by a failed suicide attempt—Kafka produced the beginnings of what many critics believe are his greatest works. In a beautifully disgusting description, Kafka told his best friend "the story came out of me like a real human birth, covered with dirt and slime." (As a front-row observer in four real human births, I can say that "dirt and slime" pretty much captures the experience.)

But then again, maybe the mess is part of the pay-off? Maybe the mess is why we feel so alive, so very *human*, in those moments when our brains finally connect the dots between slimy beginnings and beautiful creations.

3

●

LISTEN TO THE PURPLE LADY

THREE WEEKS AFTER OUR MOVE to Puerto Rico, a funny thing happened. A blackout. For the first time in thirty-nine years, the electrical grid turned off across the entire island of Puerto Rico.

Now this was a problem.

If you've ever hung out near the equator in the late summer months, you know heat and humidity are the two defining features. When the power goes out, it takes roughly six and a half minutes for everything in your refrigerator to spoil. But the thornier issue for the

parents of four young children is that your air condi-
tioners turn off.

Keep in mind that my kids were born and raised in
Minnesota. For them, the dividing line between "hot" and
"cold" is snow on the ground versus no snow on the ground.
As a result, my kids get irritable when the temperature
rises above 70 degrees. Our four-year-old, Lincoln, refuses
to get into the van on a summer day until he can see icicles
beginning to form on his baby sister's nose. But in Puerto
Rico, "hot" is measured by the liters of sweat you produce
in an hour. So just three weeks into our tropical adventure,
the absence of an air-conditioned sanctuary created some
serious irritability issues.

Fortunately, the house we're renting has a backup
generator designed to kick on automatically whenever the
power goes out. Yay!

On the day of the blackout, however, our generator did not work. Boo!

That was the problem.

Pablo held the solution.

When we moved in, the owners of our house had
mentioned that a man named Pablo comes over once a
month to service and maintain the generator. To which we
responded "OK," and then quickly moved on to the next
detail about the house. It never occurred to us to ask for
Pablo's last name, let alone his phone number or any other
piece of pertinent contact information. Honestly, it didn't

seem like a big deal. After all, it's the twenty-first century. Who needs a generator, right? Besides, our landlords were only a phone call away in Miami. When they weren't traveling, that is. When the blackout happened, they were tucked cozily into bed for the evening . . . in Scotland.

We discovered the phone number we had on file was the number for their home, thousands of miles away from Scotland. Our only choice was to send them an email, which we did. Unfortunately, our landlords have a weird habit of not checking email in their sleep.

We knew we were facing the night alone. So we dragged all the mattresses out of the boiling-hot bedrooms to the floor of the screened-in patio, where it was only simmering. We then snuggled into bed and pretended we were having a fun, old-fashioned family camp-out. On the surface of the sun.

When our landlords woke up the next morning, they checked their email and learned of our predicament. They graciously called Pablo, and asked him to come over right away. Hours later, Pablo arrived. Apparently, when the entire island is out of power, generator repair men have a fuller-than-usual schedule.

Our initial conversation with Pablo went something like this:

Nick and Alison. So glad to see you! Our generator isn't working. Can you take a look?

PABLO. **'T-:'!+""''-O>G<#@$p8^&*$%^--O.

NICK AND ALISON. Uhhh . . . *habla inglés?*

PABLO. @$%--O^^&$--O^&+_)^ *<>--O?

NICK AND ALISON. Alllll-righty then.

No matter. At least our generator speaks Spanish. That's what counted.

Pablo looked around, uttered what seemed to be a few words of encouragement, then hit a few buttons and bada-bing, bada-boom, the generator fired right up.

We shook hands. Pablo left. I went to a coffee shop to get some work done.

Twenty minutes later, Alison called me. The generator had turned off again.

LOST IN TRANSLATION

While at the coffee shop, I had randomly (and mercifully) run into the realtor who helped us find the house we were renting. Like most Puerto Ricans we've met, our realtor happens to be insanely generous and helpful. He volunteered to call Pablo to explain (in Spanish) what had happened and ask him to come back to our house.

When I got back to our house, Pablo was already there. He had the generator up and running once again.

As far as I could see, on both visits Pablo hadn't used any tools, and it had taken him less than a minute to get it going.

Now, I'm not exactly what you would call "mechanical." For most of my adult life my entire set of tools consisted of a hammer and a screwdriver in a pink plastic case labeled the "Do-it-herself toolkit." But unless Pablo was some kind of diesel-engine shaman, I was clearly missing something insanely simple. If only I knew what it was, I was confident I could do what he'd done. And if the generator stopped again, I really didn't want to be at the mercy of Pablo's work schedule or our landlord's international travel schedule. So I desperately wanted Pablo to explain the secret of his mechanical sorcery.

The problem was that, at the time, the only languages I spoke were English and Franglish. "Franglish" is the unholy linguistic mutation of English plus a handful of poorly pronounced Spanish words I had picked up, plus sprinkles of the French I'd pretended to learn in high school and college. I've since learned that Franglish is not so helpful in most conversations since the entire Franglish-speaking population of the world is yours truly. This conversation with Pablo was no exception.

So I moved on to plan B. Charades. With wildly exaggerated miming movements, I kept pointing to the generator and then doing some kind of hybrid shrug-flap movement with my arms and shoulders while chirping "*Porquoi* no working? *Porquoi* no working?" After each round of pointing, flapping, and Franglishing, Pablo would patiently say something in Spanish that made absolutely zero sense to me. So of course, I offered the only rational response when someone doesn't speak your language. I repeated the exact same thing I said before, only twice as loud.

Meanwhile, instead of joining Pablo and me in our game of multicultural charades, Alison wisely walked next door to the Purple Lady's house. The Purple Lady had been a source of endless fascination for my boys ever since we moved in. Her entire house is purple. She wears purple dresses and purple shoes every day. Her hair has purple streaks in it. Her cell phone is purple, and so is her cell-phone case, her purse, her watch and . . . well, you get the picture. She likes purple. But at this moment, the two most fascinating facts about the Purple Lady were that a) she is bilingual and b) she was graciously offering to be our interpreter.

Not a moment too soon, Alison and the Purple Lady showed up to rescue Pablo from having to endure another round of my disoriented-French-pigeon-with-Tourette's routine. Signaling that my miming services would no longer be needed, Alison gently touched my arm in the way you might caress the belly of a frazzled puppy that won't stop barking.

Finally, with the Purple Lady as our go-between, Alison and I finally heard what Pablo had been trying to tell us all along.

Your generator works. But you have to turn it on and keep it fueled.

The first time Pablo came over, the power switch was turned to the off position instead of the on position. The second time he came over, it had run out of diesel fuel.

YOUR GENERATOR WORKS

Every time a ricochet event knocks you off the power grid, you have a backup power system—a solution generator— in your mind ready and waiting to fire up. It's the same system that powers your explorer. Your mental machinery will generate flashes of insight that point the way forward just like Sarah Smith had that night in her apartment. Just like Chuck had when Ma Bell was deregulated. Just like Tim Peterson had when he walked out of that conference room. Just like I had on the drive to Minnesota.

You don't need to be creative or smart or talented or happy or rich or really, really good-looking. You don't need to be highly educated or be born into the right family in the right neighborhood or hold the right job or carry the right genetic code. You don't need to be able to run a five-minute mile, bench press a VW Beetle, have a twenty-four-inch waist, or possess sweet nunchuck skills. It doesn't matter whether you're a Mac or a PC. A generator comes standard with every human brain.

And as the Purple Lady (aka our friendly neighbor Beba) translated: *Your generator works. You just have to turn it on and keep it fueled.*

From this moment forward, if you catch yourself thinking "I'm just too much of a control freak" or "I'm too anal and type A for this loosey-goosey exploration stuff," imagine the Purple Lady telling you:

Your generator works. You just have to turn it on and keep it fueled.

If your boss delivers another unexpected blow to your sense of how things should work in the world, imagine the Purple Lady telling you:

Your generator works. You just have to turn it on and keep it fueled.

If an unexpected hospital bill or home repair shows up this week just when you thought you were getting back to a stable financial place, imagine the Purple Lady telling you:

Your generator works. You just have to turn it on and keep it fueled.

ZEN AND THE ART OF GENERATOR MAINTENANCE

You can turn your generator on whenever you like by asking four simple questions. Think of these questions as your generator-maintenance checklist. In the following chapters you'll discover more about how to use these questions and the science that explains why they work. But for right now, there's no harm in beginning to think about them:

1. A decade from now, what will you want to look back and remember doing or not doing?

2. In spite of what's happened, what practical options are you still free to pursue?

3. Even though most people would freak out in this situation, what feelings are you still free to feel, and what attitude are you still free to choose in spite of what has happened?

4. What three important things can you accomplish in the next one to three days?

4

●

REVENGE OF THE PESSIMISTS

ONCE UPON A TIME IN ANCIENT BABYLON, the goddess of chaos hooked up with the god of order. Chaos and Order produced a litter of baby gods, each one representing a different desire. As kids often do, the baby gods make a big mess of things with their careless and impulsive habits. In a disturbingly Freudian twist, the baby gods' reckless behavior culminates in the death of poor old Dad, Order. (A plot twist that feels eerily prophetic for a father of four.)

Chaos is not happy with her children. So she storms in, threatening to put some epic restrictions on screen time. In a desperate attempt to maintain unfettered access to their iPads, the baby gods go into hiding and elect their brother, the god of exploration, to protect them.

With the support of his siblings, Exploration builds up his strength and enhances his vision. (Insert action-movie training montage, replete with blindfolded sparring sessions, shirtless sprints through the desert, and lots of push-ups.) With his newly chiseled abs and super-powered eyesight, Exploration boldly confronts Chaos and vanquishes her.

He then creates a new version of Order for the world using the entrails of Chaos as his building materials for the earth and the sky.

The end.

Psychologist Jordan Peterson argues that the Enûma Eliš, the Babylonian creation myth, is much more than a superstitious fairy tale concocted by the seriously twisted ghosts of millennia past. This myth—just one variation of the same storyline found in myths from virtually every human civilization—also provides a surprisingly spot-on depiction of what goes on inside our brains whenever we face change and uncertainty.

This story is ubiquitous because the mental process it illustrates is ubiquitous.

As Peterson explains, "exploration in the face of the unknown is thus as ancient as hunger, thirst, sex, and aggression. It is a primary drive."

Your brain, my brain, and everyone else's brain is wired to generate solutions to chaos through a finely tuned mental process of exploration.

Like a game of cosmic rock-paper-scissors, the story of your brain on change follows three simple rules:

> *Chaos replaces order.*
> *Exploration replaces chaos.*
> *New order (order, version 2.0) replaces exploration.*

Whenever I find myself struggling with change, it's almost always because I'm ignoring the pattern. I'm trying to conquer the chaos by vainly attempting to restore the old order.

In 2007, it took me a long time to wrap my head around the fact that the old order—the one I knew so well and grew so attached to—was dead. I didn't live in San Diego anymore. I couldn't go surfing every day anymore. My wife and I weren't newlyweds with complete and total control over our schedule anymore. I didn't have a fun office filled with coworkers anymore. The old order was dead. It wasn't napping. It wasn't on vacation. It wasn't taking a long lunch break. It was *dead*. D-E-A-D. *Dead.*

I had forgotten that chaos will eventually replace order. At work. At home. With your health. With your future. In society. In the marketplace. Every single time.

That might sound pessimistic and hopeless. But Salvatore Maddi and countless other researchers over the last half century have consistently found that people who expect life to have challenges and hiccups not only cope better with stressful changes, they actually live longer. In other words, expecting a certain amount of chaos in your life makes you mentally and physically healthier.

For people like Chuck, the "good life" is measured in units of meaning. It looks like an exciting adventure story with mountains to scale, fellow travelers to befriend, people to rescue, and fears to conquer. A good day for Chuck was one in which he chose to do something meaningful in response to whatever happens to him.

When you're thinking like Andy, you measure the "good life" in units of happiness. For Andy, the ideal life resembles a pleasure cruise. He expects every day to be planned by a world-class event coordinator who anticipates his every need and promises zero surprises when the bill comes. A good day for Andy is a day with no unexpected wrinkles or inconveniences. Andy and two-thirds of his coworkers viewed Ma Bell's changes as some kind of tragic anomaly—the kind of thing that happened only to a tiny percentage of unfortunate souls like them. So instead of setting their minds free to explore the options for a new future, they kept their brains chained to the rotting carcass of yesterday's order and hiding under the cold, yet comforting, shadow of old goals, outdated processes, self-defeating habits, unforgiven offenses, and coworkers who fed off their mutual misery.

They forgot that the next rule of change is equally as powerful. That rule says that exploration defeats chaos. Every single time. We just have to remember to set our explorers free.

TRAGIC OPTIMISM

One day in August 1945, an Austrian physician named Viktor Frankl was finally sent home from the Nazi death camps that had been his prison since 1942. As if being teased by death and surrounded by suffering day after day for three straight years wasn't punishment enough, Frankl now discovered that his mother, his father, his brother, his young wife, their unborn child, and most of his closest friends had all died horrible deaths.

The hospital he worked at had been reduced to rubble.

The manuscript of the book he was writing—his life's work—had been stripped from him right along with the shirt off his back the day he arrived at the camps.

Everything in his life had changed. All he loved was lost.

But as fall became winter and winter gave way to spring, Frankl began to discover something else. Even though he could never go back to the life he once had, he was still free to meet new friends, to marry a new wife, to father a new child, to work with new patients, to enjoy music and read books.

Frankl concluded that even though you and I are never free from fate, we are always free to decide how we respond to it. We are always free to explore new options. That freedom can never be taken from us.

Never *free from* change.

Always *free to* decide.

This is the central idea of something Viktor Frankl labeled "tragic optimism." Tragic optimism says fate and freedom are two sides of the same coin. It's up to each of us to choose which side we focus on.

Tragic optimism doesn't ask you to assume everything will always work out for the best or that everything happens for some unknown reason. In fact, that might be one of the most tragic misinterpretations of tragic optimism.

Frankl is probably best known for the idea that we can always "find meaning in our suffering."

But what he really meant is that we can find something meaningful to live for in the midst of our struggle. Even though we are never free from death, cancer, layoffs, paralysis, or concentration camps, we are always free to provide a meaningful response. In other words, we should look for a reason not to fold. We should try to find a reason why we should *endure* the suffering—because there is a person still to be loved or a work still to be finished or a moral victory still to be won. That's a very different thing than finding a *reason why* our suffering is happening.

Frankl clearly states how the worst thing about the concentration camps was how everything that happened in the camps—who got to eat and who didn't, who was beaten and when and why—was completely arbitrary and pointless. But he wasn't arguing that the event itself—*being sent to a concentration camp*—was somehow meaningful.

This simple distinction can prevent us from wasting years of our lives wandering down a dead-end road asking questions that have no answers.

Here's a fun fact: one huge study in the late 1990s found that the majority of people who get grief therapy after some tragic event fail to improve at all. Two out of five people actually get *worse* after the grief counseling sessions.

Why?

Because reliving a troubling event again and again by reexamining it every week—in a misguided attempt to find some meaningful reason why it happened—often just throws gas on the fire. It is as likely to lead to rumination and chronic depression as it is to inspire some kind of breakthrough. Of course every person and every situation is unique. I spoke to some people who said that grief counseling was exactly what they needed—the only thing that helped them was talking about their situation with other people who had gone through a similar event. I also talked to other people who said that group therapy only reinforced their depression. Research pretty clearly demonstrates that grieving has no one-size-fits-all solution.

My point here is simply this: when you accept the fact that *shift happens*—that chaos replaces order—it can recalibrate your expectations for how the world is supposed to work and help liberate you from a maze of unanswerable questions. You can start exploring options for a new future rather than handcuffing yourself to the old order. You can turn your attention to the question of: *What meaningful things am I still free to do in spite of what happened?*

Asking that question is how you fire up your generator.

YOUR DECISION POINT

During a single one-month period, a friend of mine broke up with his girlfriend, lost his job of twelve years, and was forced to move out of the apartment he had lived in for ten years. When I talked to him a few months later, this normally kind and sensitive guy explained how "all the people who told me 'this is a great opportunity' . . . I wanted to punch 'em in the throat."

As a general rule, I prefer not to get throat-punched. So I'm not going to tell you that whatever change or adversity you're going through right now is a "great opportunity." Even if you don't karate chop my esophagus, I know from experience that this chestnut of reassurance usually smacks headfirst into rolling eyes, folded arms, and clenched teeth. The loss of a loved one or an unexpected layoff or an upsetting reorg or the onset of a new disease or winding up in a Nazi death camp are all ricochet events that hurt.

I don't know you. I don't have the foggiest idea whether you're experiencing a minor irritation or taking a detour through Dante's Ninth Circle of Hell.

What I can say with absolute certainty is that nobody can change what has already happened. Like it or not. Regret what you did. Resent what happened to you in spite of your best efforts. None of that matters anymore. It happened. It's done. But no matter what, you're still 100 percent free to decide what to do next.

Let me be blunt. You're at a decision point.

You can choose to fixate on your inability to control the decisions of your bosses, your competitors, your customers, your partner, Mother Nature, God Almighty, or the invisible hand of the market. You can keep going back in time to try to explain who or what is responsible for your sad state. If you make that choice, you will inevitably succumb to worry, bitterness, and despair.

Instead, you can choose to accept the reality that shift happens. You can choose to focus your energy on the fact that you are always—*always, always, always*—free to decide how you will respond to what happens to you. If you make that choice, I can promise you that your brain and this book will help you craft a response that will give you legitimate reason to hope. Not some hokey fairy tale. But a real strategy for a real future.

The secret of every highly adaptive person is that sooner or later, they stop searching for explanations and start searching for a way forward. It might take a day, a week, a month, or multiple years for that shift to happen. But eventually, their search for meaning shifts from the past to the future. That's when the true adventure begins.

Is today that day for you?

PART 2

PURSUE PROGRESS

5

•

BE THE CHUCK YOU WANT TO SEE IN THE WORLD

We don't run from the bear because we are afraid. We are afraid because we run from the bear.

—William James

WHEN THABISO ROWAN (pronounced *tuh*-BEE-*so*) opened his eyes for the first time in three weeks, the twenty-six-year-old musician remembered nothing about climbing up his favorite tree, the one with the panoramic view of the Mississippi River. As he rested there scanning his sterile, white surroundings, questions flooded his mind. Why am I in this hospital bed? How did I get here? Why won't my legs move?

Over the next few months, the avid runner laid there helpless, trying to absorb the reality that he would never walk again. Then he lost his job. Then his car. Then his girlfriend. Then his home.

An even darker set of questions now crept in and slowly overshadowed his once-optimistic outlook. Why did this happen? What's the point in trying? Is living another day even worth it?

But then he remembered something that changed everything. One day shortly after his accident, while he was still in the hospital, an anonymous nurse came into his room to check his medications. After a few moments, she stopped and looked at him.

"It's not about the hundreds of things you can't do," she said. "It's about the thousands of things you can do." Then she walked out the door, and he never saw her again.

Today, Thabiso is one of the most refreshing people you'll ever meet—funny without being naïve, upbeat without being obnoxious. But that's not because he regained the use of his legs. Or because his girlfriend came back. Or because he got back his old job, his old car, or his old home.

The only thing that changed was where he decided to focus—not on the work, the home, the relationships, and the future plans he had forever lost; but on the work, the home, the relationships, and the future plans still out there.

It's a perfect example of Frankl's tragic optimism.

But, here's the twist. Thabiso didn't remember this piece of life-changing advice until almost six months later. When that nurse told him that, he told me, "I was just sitting there watching TV in the hospital, all doped up on pain meds, probably drooling on myself. I probably just grunted."

So why did this encounter all of the sudden come back to him months later?

In the months that followed his release from the hospital, depression kicked in as the reality of his new life became clearer. Thabiso told me "the worst part was seeing my mom and my aunties so sad. I couldn't take it. So I pretended to be happy. I just kept telling them 'no need to be sad, everything will be OK,' even though I really wasn't sure if *I* believed that everything would be OK."

FAKE IT 'TIL YOU MAKE IT

If I told you to impersonate a depressed person, what would you do? You'd probably slump your shoulders, sag your head, slouch your back, put on a sad face with droopy eyelids and a frowning mouth. You would probably talk and walk a little slower. By doing that, your posture would send your brain a message. Your brain would process the available information—slumped shoulders, low-slung head, droopy eyes, frowny face—and conclude, *yep, we're sad; we should probably lie down*. And since now you're lying down, your brain says, *we must not have any energy*, which further confirms the initial diagnosis of sadness. Then in order to make sense of our sudden sadness, our explorer would go searching its memory files for other memories of conversations and events that might piece together a story that explains why we're sad.

If I told you to act like an energetic and outgoing person, the opposite happens. Now your brain starts seeking evidence to explain why you feel so vibrant, so it recalls related events that might explain our jovial mood. In one study, researchers asked introverted people to act extroverted. Even though the introverts were fully aware that they were just *pretending* to be gregarious people, they later scored significantly higher on measures of happiness.

When Thabiso decided to pretend to be happy for the sake of his family members, he started smiling more and sitting up straighter. When people asked him how he was doing, he started saying things like "I'm great!" instead of "oh, ya know, getting by, I guess." And all of these fake words and fabricated gestures started to send a very real new message to his brain. His brain took the hint and concluded, *hmm, I guess we must be happy now*—which then triggered his brain to explain this newfound happiness. Only then did it access a long forgotten memory file for "reasons to be joyful." That's where it eventually uncovered the nurse's nugget of wisdom about it not being "about the hundreds of things you can't do, but the thousands of things you can do."

PARENT TRAP

Comedian Jim Gaffigan once explained, "If you want to know what it's like to have four kids, just imagine that you're drowning . . . and someone hands you a baby."

One day, a couple of years ago, my wife Alison was drowning.

It was just months after our daughter, Gwendolyn (baby number four), was born. Our normally docile baby girl inexplicably demanded that Alison hold her every single second of that day. Our three-year-old son, Lincoln, had simultaneously decided temper tantrums would be his default response to anything and everything that happened within earshot of him that day.

Meanwhile, our older sons, Franklin and Rueben, were in the backyard playing soccer. Suddenly Alison heard our oldest son wailing. He came running into the house holding his mouth and looking for Mom. Apparently he had fallen into the well of the egress window in our backyard. It turned out he wasn't hurt that bad, but he did chip his tooth.

The chipped tooth was the proverbial straw that nearly snapped the back of Alison's sanity that day.

I was already in the process of researching *Ricochet* at that time, and since I tend to leave my research materials strategically placed (by which I mean randomly scattered) all around the house, Alison had picked up one of Viktor Frankl's books earlier that week. She remembered reading Frankl's quote about the one freedom that can never be taken from us, "the last of the human freedoms—the freedom to choose one's attitude."

Since she pretty much had nothing to lose at that point, she thought, *Meh, why not give it a try?*

She decided she was going to choose an attitude of peace and contentment vis-à-vis the complete and utter poo storm in which she was neck deep. Much to her surprise, it worked.

When she felt like raising her voice, she forced herself to smile instead. When the orthodontist's office put her on hold for twenty minutes, instead of huffing and puffing she took a deep breath and forced a big, fake, toothy smile. When our toddler screamed for her in the other room, instead of stomping in to ask what he wanted, Alison walked slowly into the other room with a gentle smile on her face.

At first it took every ounce of strength she had to contort her livid expressions into half-baked smiles. But eventually, she confessed, they started coming naturally. Just like when Thabiso started pretending to be happy and then remembered that nurse's advice, Alison's forced contentment unearthed the memory of a friend telling her that if you look at your life as a pie chart, the period of time when you'll have little kids is really just a sliver on that big pie—maybe five to ten years of an eighty-year whole. That thought then led to a flood of *unforced* gratitude and appreciation, which produced genuine smiles, which reinforced the sense of peace and contentment.

In fact, it worked so well that Alison has even applied a similar technique to our three sons.

Recently, the boys began going through a phase where they were constantly fighting with each other. Since I also grew up as one of three brothers, I told my wife this phase for little boys has a name: *childhood*. But for some reason she refused to believe that *her* little boys were savage beasts by nature like my brothers and I were (are?). So she instituted a rule that whenever our sons hit each other, they won't get a stern talking-to or TV restrictions or a whoopin'. For punishment, they have to hug each other.

Sure enough, every time they hug each other they can't help laughing. Why? Our minds just can't handle the inconsistency of an "angry hug." The forced behavior creates a genuine emotion.

That's the secret of choosing your attitude.

When we choose to be strong or peaceful or bold or energetic, we don't immediately become strong or peaceful or bold or energetic. That's why people sometimes write off the strategy as a simplistic solution that just doesn't work. And they're not entirely wrong; it isn't a sudden transformation. It works because it sets off a chain reaction. Our conscious choice changes our words and our posture and our facial expressions. Which sends cues to our mind. From there, our minds will take over.

It's sort of like jump-starting a car with a dead battery. You can't just snap your fingers and make the car start. You have to hook up the cables and manually give it a little juice to get it going. But once you have the car started, the systems in your engine will take over and you won't need the jumper cables anymore. Our minds are wired to work the same way. They are basically set up to do exactly what they need to do to help you adapt. Sometimes you just have to give them a little jump-start.

That's why choosing an adaptive attitude is where act two begins for every story of successful adaptation you'll ever hear. When you choose an adaptive attitude, your brain starts paying more attention to Chuck's advice than Andy's advice.

This is as true for leadership decisions made in response to slumping sales, economic downturns, and industry shake-ups as it is for life decisions made in response to tragic accidents, devastating diagnoses, and shattered marriages.

ACCIDENTAL ANDYS

When you act like a Chuck, your brain gives you ammunition to support your *Chuck-ness*.

When you act like an Andy, just the opposite happens. But most of the time we don't even realize we're emanating *Andy-ness*.

After analyzing some of my own self-tormenting tendencies and carefully observing thousands of workers in organizations all over the world, I've compiled this list of nine hidden habits that are virtually guaranteed to bring out the Andy in you:

1. Keep your eyes ready to roll. When skillfully deployed, the eye roll is a cynic's most versatile weapon. Whether on a conference call or in a status meeting, a simple ocular rotation will keep your feet firmly planted in a pit of hopeless despair by reminding you how pointless your job is and how superior you are to the silly duties and ignorant people surrounding you.

2. Expect your leaders to qualify for sainthood. If your boss doesn't possess the compassion of Mother Theresa, the team-building skills of Abraham Lincoln, and the innovative genius of Steve Jobs, then he clearly isn't fit for middle management. Somewhere over the rainbow is the divinely perfect boss you're entitled to. Until that angelic leader reveals herself, true virtuosos of vitriol will tolerate nothing less than perfection from all the schlubs they work for.

3. Assume your coworkers are incompetent. Obviously, it's not fair to hold your coworkers to the same high standards as your boss. So when a mix-up happens with a colleague, instead of assuming your team members are bad people, be the bigger person and just assume they're stupid.

4. Eat lunch with people who hate their job. Occasionally, in moments of weakness, you might catch yourself thinking your bosses and your peers are decent, hard-working people doing the best they can. This kind of thinking seriously threatens the pursuit of misery. That's why it's important to regularly associate with people who can remind you of everything imperfect about your job, your coworkers, and your organization.

5. Expect heaps of praise for every act of slightly above-average performance. People committed to misery know that pay and recognition are the only reasons to do good work. Some naïve saps will tell you that the satisfaction of doing a job well provides its own valuable reward. But miserable people know better. That's why they always expect praise and make sure to be outraged anytime they don't receive it.

6. Interpret every inconvenience as a personal assault on your health and happiness. Sometimes tasks fall through the cracks. Sometimes people get caught up in the heat of the moment and say things they regret. When these things happen, you could be forgiving and understanding. But why? It will be much easier to achieve martyrdom by clinging to the belief that everyone is conspiring to ruin your life.

7. Smile sparingly and never laugh. Everyone knows that if you act cheerful more than 10 percent of the time, people might think you're one of those conformist sheep who actually likes their job. If you're not careful, these wanton acts of pleasure can signal approval of your work environment while seriously diminishing your street cred with the wretched souls you should be eating lunch with every day. (*Note: Disapproving smirks are acceptable as long as they don't spill into something resembling a genuine smile.*)

8. Complain about how screwed up things are, and then complain more when someone tries to change them. If you look hard enough, no executive's decision is above reproach. This is especially true for change decisions. Whenever you disagree with your leader's judgment, instead of giving her the benefit of the doubt, just assume she's a spawn of Satan who stays up until the wee hours of the morning stroking her barbed-tail while scheming about ways to destroy the company and poison your happiness.

9. If you can't be condescending, at least be indignant. Some people are gifted at channeling their contempt for others into smug replies and condescending facial expressions. Other people are better suited to moral outrage and righteous indignation. Both skills can produce misery equally well, so be yourself! If arrogance is your thing, then mumble sarcastic comments under your breath. If self-righteousness is your bag, then turn minor offenses into holy wars. The key is to be *authentic* in your misery.

Expressing tolerance of other people's shortcomings and gratitude for the gifts you have been given is no way to eke out a miserable existence. But if you decide you'd rather not clock in at Dante's *Inferno* tomorrow morning, take a deep breath, crack a smile, and pick one of these habits to break this week. Your friends and family will thank you.

6

•

BACK TO THE FUTURE

Where we're going, we don't need roads.

—Doc Brown in *Back to the Future*

WHEN CARMEN WALKED THROUGH the front door after work that night, Kevin could see the news written on her face. She didn't need to say it. But she did, anyway.

"Well, it finally happened. They eliminated my position."

Without being able to find the right words to say, Kevin just looked at her with that genuinely sympathetic expression Carmen knew so well. It was the look she always got when she brought bad news home from work. It was the same look she had gotten four years ago when a reorg kicked her out of the finance department.

It was that look she dreaded most. She knew Kevin's concern was sincere. But she always felt like that look of sympathy was masking something else. Like it was covering up a feeling of disappointment. That's what she hated the most. Not the uncertainty about the future. Not the sudden financial concerns. It was the sense of shame she felt whenever she disappointed the people around her.

"Twenty-nine years—my entire career—at that place and this is the thanks I get."

She barely slept the next few weeks as a jumble of fears and frustrations bounced around her brain every time she closed her eyes. Since they wouldn't be announcing her position elimination for another month, Carmen did her best to put on a happy face and pretend like everything was OK as she drifted through her meetings that week.

But then one weekend something changed.

Carmen and Kevin were at a cocktail party and one of their friends shared that a similar misfortune had befallen him. After years of dedicated service to his employer, this friend had also gotten the boot just a few months earlier. He was still radiating bitterness. After feverishly working to land another job, he had found a new position. But this one was even worse than his old job, which only amplified the bitterness he felt about his layoff.

On the drive home that night, Carmen had a revelation.

"Without realizing it," she later told me, "I had started slipping into this woe-is-me attitude. I knew it wasn't personal, and that I just wasn't in vogue at the moment. But it was just really hard not to take it personally. It was like 'twenty-nine years and now *this?*' But it wasn't until talking to our friend that I saw my attitude manifested in him." She smiled. "He was like my ghost of Christmas future or something."

The next morning, Carmen woke up and asked herself a question. *Carmen, you've got another eight to ten years of work left in you. When you look back on this situation at the end of that time, how do you want to remember handling this?*

When we ask ourselves a question like that a funny thing happens. We start to worry less, and work more.

THIS TOO SHALL PASS

In a recent series of experiments, researchers at the University of California, Berkeley prompted some people to think about how flopping a presentation, bombing a test, losing a client or falling victim to some other every-day calamity will have lasting implications for their future.

They then prompted a second group to adopt a this-too-shall-pass attitude by asking them to think about how the things that bring us down today often mean very little to us a few years down the road. Not surprisingly, this second group was an average of 24 percent less worried and depressed than the first group.

But the big discovery was this: the people in the this-too-shall-pass group were also 16 percent more likely to attack the distressing problem.

Did you catch that?

Maybe you should read it again, because it's easy to miss.

The people who were able to look at their problem and conclude *ya know, I guess it's not really that big of a deal in the big picture of things* didn't ignore the problem. They were actually *more likely* to confront the problem head on.

We've all been conditioned to believe that when you have a team to lead, a family to feed, or goals to meet, taking a no-worries-bro attitude is downright irresponsible. That's probably why you don't often see corporate executives sporting "Keep Calm & Carry On" T-shirts when they announce a reorg or less-than-stellar quarterly earnings.

But the truth is that keeping setbacks and challenges in perspective isn't irresponsible. It's effective—because it creates a healthy distance. It helps us step outside the emotionally overwhelmed present and see the situation more accurately.

That also means we can still be responsible citizens, good parents, high performers, and diligent managers without spending our days worrying, and our nights and weekends feeling guilty about *not* worrying.

WHAT WOULD CARMEN DO?

When you look back on this situation ten years from now, what will you regret saying or doing? What will you regret not doing?

When Carmen asked herself this question, it triggered a conversation between her present self and her future self:

PRESENT CARMEN. I'm pissed off. If I weren't trying to be a good Christian woman about the whole thing, there were a lot of people I'd like to share some choice expletives with.

FUTURE CARMEN. Don't make enemies.

PRESENT CARMEN. I hate being in this place of not knowing what's going to happen. I hate going to work every day feeling like a failure. I need to get another job ASAP so I can get out of this funk.

FUTURE CARMEN. Be patient. You aren't desperate
             for money and your next job could be
             the one you've always wanted.

Don't make enemies. Hold out for *the* job you want. Those
became Carmen's guiding principles for her months in the
fog.

    When she got the urge to jump on the first job
offer that came her way, her future self reminded her, *Be
patient. Buy yourself some time.* So she started contacting
colleagues she had known over the years to see about doing
temporary projects within the organization, which would
give her more time to find the *right* position. Even though
her position had been eliminated, she was still free to put
those twenty-eight years of acquired knowledge to use for
someone else—especially since so many people were sub-
stantially overworked thanks to the mass layoffs.

    Every time she felt tempted to tell off her former
boss, her future self reminded her "don't make enemies."
Every time her former team members and coworkers
mentioned how it just didn't seem fair that she, of all
people, had lost her job, and she got the urge to tell them
how she really felt about the raw deal she'd been given,
her future self showed up again to remind her "don't
make enemies."

    When I caught up with Carmen a year after her
position had been eliminated, she had landed her dream

job—the one she'd wanted when she first started her career. She was happier at work than she had been in years.

"I can say now [the layoff] was one of the *better* things that's happened to me . . . not quite the best thing yet, but I'm moving in that direction."

Just maybe, every now and again bad things truly do happen for a good reason? Hmm . . . .

But enough of that happy and hopeful talk. Let's think about how bad it could actually get.

THE WORRY WALL

"I don't know how much longer I can do this," Jared said to me behind an uncomfortable smirk that betrayed his prolonged state of barely manageable panic. Nearing his fortieth birthday, Jared seemed to be the embodiment of the everyday person's American Dream. His mother had passed away when he was young. During his entire child-hood, his restless father had a hard time holding down a job for more than a few months at a time, which meant Jared's youth was geographically nomadic, emotionally unstable, and materially deprived. Yet in spite of his rocky start to life, Jared found his dream girl—with whom he had three beautiful kids, ages ten, eight, and six—and he worked his way into the leadership ranks of a global bank.

A little more than a year before our talk, things started to change at work for Jared. His European-based company was reorganizing—moving ever more authority away from Jared's office back to the headquarters in Europe. As a result, Jared was gradually forced to cut his staff head count and accept what was ostensibly a lateral move within the organization. But it felt suspiciously similar to a demotion since he no longer reported directly to the president. All this, even though just four years earlier he'd been tapped as one of only eight high-potential managers to receive special training for an eventual executive role.

After the reorg, a competing company headquartered just down the street from his current office offered Jared a new, higher-ranking position. After much deliberation, he accepted the job with the competitor along with its corresponding pay raise and title boost. In many respects, it was Jared's dream job. The problem was that on top of his new company's vast cultural differences, the organization was mired in chaos. It was taking its toll on him.

Although Jared had initially been a consulting client, we became friends over the years and our conversations tended to shift effortlessly and frequently between the personal and the professional. So when he said he couldn't take it anymore, I had to clarify if he was talking about work or home.

Even though his new office was just blocks away from his former office, Jared and his wife had decided to downsize their home and move closer to the city to reduce Jared's commute. Although it cut down his travel time, moving closer to the city put his kids in a new school and increased their mortgage even though they bought an older and a smaller house than the one they had lived in before.

As a result, his acute stress at work was compounded by acute stress at home.

After listening to Jared explain how he was trapped in a tangled web of personal and professional turmoil, I walked him through what I call the "and then what?" exercise. The dialogue went like this:

ME. Let's assume this job not only *doesn't* get better, it actually gets worse. What will happen?

JARED. I'll probably get fired.

ME. And then what?

JARED. Well, depending on how long it takes me to find another job, we'd probably have to sell our house, or let it get foreclosed.

ME. And assuming you can't find another job for a year or longer. Then what?

JARED. Then Kelly would probably have to go back to work teaching.

ME. Finding a teaching job around here these days doesn't seem all that easy or at least quick. Assuming she can't find a job. Then what?

JARED. I don't know. I guess then we'd probably end up moving back to Tampa, maybe even move in with Kelly's parents.

ME. And then what?

JARED. Actually, it's funny you mention it. My dad has been managing a restaurant for almost five years now. The owner and all the customers love him, so he wants my dad to take it over. Working with him at a restaurant in Tampa where Kelly could be close to her family again sounds really appealing right now. Peaceful, actually.

ME. Yeah, I could definitely see that. So on the one hand, you get the dream job figured out and you get to stay in Atlanta. On the other hand, the job situation goes all to hell. You get canned. You lose your house, and then have move close to your families, where your kids can see their grandparents every day and you get to work with your dad in a lower-stress environment

that allows you to see your kids more
often, which is something you desperately want. Does that sound about right?

JARED. (*smiling*) Yeah, I guess that's about it.
Doesn't sound too bad either way, does it?

Asking the and-then-what questions usually leads to break-
ing the worry wall. The worry wall is a self-made barrier
between you and a chain of events that seems so dreadful
you can't even bear to think about it. Brick by brick, we
build up this wall to protect us from the what-ifs that are
just too scary to really consider.

But as the wall gets higher, we lose sight of the fact
that most possible scenarios on the other side of the wall
really aren't as dreadful as we've made them out to be. The
string of and-then-what questions is sort of like pulling
yourself up, inch by inch, to the top of the wall—where
you can finally see for yourself that there are still plenty
of opportunities for a happy and meaningful life even if
something really does trigger this frightening chain of
events. You can see that even those scenarios are different,
they also offer unique advantages that aren't possible in
your current situation.

Jared isn't alone here. We all build worry walls. It's
our mind's way of trying to protect us from uncomfortable uncertainties.

I am no exception. Since I haven't been the recipient of a regular paycheck in almost eight years, during which time I've also added new mouths to feed at a pace that would make most rabbits blush, I go through this and-then-what series of questions every few months. It's my way of talking myself *onto* the ledge of my worry wall. I take a good look, conclude once again that it's not so bad either way, and then shimmy back down the rope and get back to work.

COLLATERAL INSPIRATION

An unexpected bonus of Carmen's guiding principles was the impact her attitude had on her former team members. They later confided that they all marveled at how gracefully she responded to her setback. In the months that followed, many of those same people were also displaced and shuffled around. When their own ricochet events happened, they said Carmen was their role model for how to react.

So what about you? Ten years from now, when you look back on this situation what might you regret doing or saying? What will you regret *not* doing or saying? When your coworkers tell the story of what happened to you, what do you want them to say about how you responded? When you tell your kids the story of what happened to you, what character-building lessons would you like to illustrate for them?

Will you tell a hard luck story about how the world took a big, steamy dump on you that you didn't deserve, and so you rolled over and waited to die?

Will you tell a revenge fantasy that culminates with you walking into your boss's office, telling him off, and maybe even relieving yourself in the potted plant on his windowsill? And let's not forget the part about spending the next ten years regretting your actions.

Or will you tell a triumphant story about how you got hit hard, but then astonished everyone by refusing to let your hope die in spite of wave after wave of challenge and adversity?

Ultimately, your choice comes down to this: Ten years from now, do you want your friends and your kids and your coworkers to feel sorry for you?

Or do you want your friends or your kids and your coworkers to be inspired by how heroically you responded to tough circumstances?

7

•

LIVIN' ON A PRAYER

She says: We've gotta hold on to what we've got.

—Jon Bon Jovi

ONCE UPON A TIME, not so long ago, my wife and I woke up at two in the morning. We pulled our one-year-old, four-year-old, seven-year-old, and nine-year-old out of a deep slumber and hurriedly carried them into a preloaded cargo van. I instructed the driver to go straight to the nearest airstrip. If we were lucky, there would be a plane waiting for us. This was the moment of truth. Eighteen months of planning came down to this early-morning rendezvous. Luckily, thanks no doubt to divine intervention, fourteen hours after our journey began we finally touched down in San Juan.

Little did I know the adventure was only beginning.

OK, since the "driver" was my buddy Jedd and the "airstrip" was the newly renovated Minneapolis–St. Paul Airport, it wasn't exactly like we were refugees fleeing an unstable dictatorship under the cover of night. However, in-flight movies and meal service notwithstanding, managing twelve hours of air travel with two sleep-deprived toddlers is a harrowing adventure of another kind. (And I still say divine intervention is the only reasonable explanation for the on-time departure of our connecting flight out of Chicago O'Hare.)

But this transition really was the beginning of an adventure.

Before arriving in San Juan on September 1, we had spent a grand total of four days in Puerto Rico. We'd never been to the city we were moving to (Ponce) or even the region in which it was located (the south)—let alone set eyes on the house or driven through the neighborhood in which we would be living for the next year. Although the Duolingo app on my phone claimed I was 21 percent fluent in Spanish before I arrived, I quickly discovered that knowing the Spanish words for *bear* and *dog* and *bathroom* isn't especially useful when trying to explain to a taxi driver where an obscure shipping dock is in a city you've never been to, or while trying to ask a Spanish-speaking government clerk why you unexpectedly owe an additional $1,800 in excise taxes on the vehicle you just paid $2,000 to ship. Not to mention buy gas, read road signs, find ketchup at the grocery story, or do pretty much anything at all at the department of motor vehicles.

A pre-arrival phone miscommunication with an extremely helpful sales rep at the Rent-A-Center left us with no furniture, no dishware, and no utensils for the first week we lived there.

No less than three days into our adventure, I also lost my wallet—including driver's license, credit cards, debit cards, and basically any other source of funding. And since there are no Wells Fargo branches in Puerto Rico, accessing money to do simple things like purchase basic household necessities, food, and gas, as well as setting up an Internet connection, suddenly became even more complicated. On top of all that, add an inconsistent water supply (*Shower? Oops, not today, I guess.*), plus a freak island-wide blackout, plus a still-unsolved mystery about why not even one of four different Internet providers can connect our house to the World Wide Web, and what do you get?

You either get a surefire recipe for an anxiety attack or an excellent illustration of something I call the "control cliff."

THE CONTROL CLIFF

Time and again, research shows that the people who most successfully overcome setbacks and plow through uncertain changes are the people who feel the greatest sense of control over the outcomes in their life. On the other hand, it's plain to see that some events—economic dips, corporate layoffs, natural disasters, and bad hair days—truly are out of our control.

Which begs the question: Are we free or not?

Are the most resilient and adaptive people ignorant of reality? For the rest of us to become more resilient, must we choke down a sugary blend of naïveté and delusion?

Actually, no. The truth reveals a strange paradox. Resilient people retain their sense of control by acknowledging their lack of control.

It works like this: When an unexpected or unwanted change happens, it's as if resilient people draw a horizontal line. Above that line, they list uncontrollable issues. Below the line, they list controllable issues:

Uncontrollable Issues

- The economy could tank.
- My customers could buy less from me.
- My leaders could order a new round of layoffs.
- The Donald/Hillary could win the election.
- The cancer could come back.
- My partner could leave me.

Controllable Issues

- How I choose to allocate my available budget dollars.
- How much effort I expend each day trying to serve my customers' needs.
- Who I choose to vote for.
- What I eat and how often I visit my doctor.
- How I choose to treat my partner.

I call that horizontal line the control cliff. Resilient people don't just think about these two sets of issues differently. They respond to them differently.

They give the controllable issues a *fix-and-focus treatment*. They create action plans to solve the problems they can *fix*, and they *focus* their goals exclusively on opportunities that are within their power to realize.

In contrast, they give uncontrollable issues a *hope-and-pray treatment*. In order to preserve their priceless sense of control, resilient people hand those uncontrollable hopes and fears over to statistical probability or to Mother Nature or to God or to whatever higher power holds dominion in their worldview.

They then get back to work fixing the problems, and focusing on the goals, that they *can* control. That approach leads to noticeable progress. Which leads to increased confidence. Which leads to greater effort. Which leads to better outcomes. Which leads to a world that suddenly feels more controllable as well as more hopeful.

Anxiety happens when we drive over the edge of the control cliff—when we start trying to give the fix-and-focus treatment to issues over which we have no control.

If this is all starting to sound familiar, it's because this is basically the scientific rationale for the widely known Serenity Prayer written by the theologian Reinhold Niebuhr. It goes like this "God, grant me the serenity to accept the things I cannot change; courage to change the things I can; and wisdom to know the difference." You've probably heard it before. I had heard it numerous times. I always liked it in theory. But I struggled to put that idea into practice until I started really digging into the empirical research on our perceptions of control. I'll let you decide whether that makes me a good social scientist or a bad Christian. Either way, at some point during the past decade's hurricane of change, I've found that framing the Serenity Prayer in terms of the control cliff has made it easier to apply. I think it has something to do with the visual imagery of a cliff's edge separating sturdy ground from a vast cavern and open sky.

Now anytime I start to feel anxious about something, I simply ask myself *which side of the control cliff is it on?*

RED BALLOONS GO BY

The grocery store in our old neighborhood had a jar of free balloons for kids sitting at the checkout counter. So whenever my kids came to the store with me as toddlers, they would dig a paw into the plastic jar and grab a balloon. I would blow it up, tie it off, and hand it to them.

As sure as the sun rises, they would immediately walk out to the parking lot, get distracted, forget they were holding a balloon, and let it go. Then they would release a torrent of shocked and anguished tears as if it were the first time in recorded history that a balloon ever had the audacity to drift up to the clouds and go bye-bye forever.

Precisely three and a half minutes later they would completely forget the balloon ever existed.

We are free to consciously treat boneheaded mistakes and cosmic hiccups the same way toddlers accidentally treat balloons. We can blow it up, tie it off, and let it go. We may have to endure a brief surge of anxiety, but then we can move on to fixing and focusing on the things we have some control over.

When I lose my wallet, I can curse the heavens. I can stomp my feet. I can try to blame my wife, my kids, my congressmen, my neighbors, my doctors, my parents, my overbearing third-grade teacher, evil spirits, terrorists, televisions, video games, or the Elf on the Shelf. I can torture myself with guilt, shame, worry, and regret. But none of that will allow me to change what's already happened.

Or I can let the mistake drift to the clouds and identify the steps I can actually take to resolve the issue. I can check my credit card accounts to see if any transactions have been made and call the credit card companies to order replacements, and begin the absurdly long eight-week process of retrieving an out-of-state driver's license replacement.

I can't make all government officials in Puerto Rico speak English (which is sort of an absurd expectation to begin with) so I don't chase that issue over the edge of the control cliff. I take it to the edge, tie it up, and watch it go bye-bye. Then I examine what I can do. I can ramp up my efforts to learn Spanish more quickly by practicing at restaurants and grocery stores while solving the immediate issues by humbly asking for help from the handful of insanely generous bilingual people we have already met.

For some reason, my neighbors on both sides of us can connect to the Internet, but six weeks and four very frustrated installers later, I have to conclude that cable TV and in-home Wi-Fi are just not in the cards for us. So up, up, and away that issue goes, drifting peacefully over the horizon.

But Alison and I do have hot spots on our mobile phones. Even though we had never used them before, we *could* control whether or not we start using them. Which then led us to the uncontrollable issue of Sprint's dreadful connectivity inside our cement house. What I could control was the choice to switch from Sprint to AT&T, which miraculously has much better connectivity. We then beefed up our data package with the money we would have spent every month on cable and Internet.

It's not perfect. But it is all part of the adventure.

8

●

THE MARTIAN PLAN

*At some point, everything's gonna go south on you . . . everything's
going to go south and you're going to say, this is it. This is how I
end. Now you can either accept that, or you can get back to work.
That's all it is. You just begin. You do the math. You solve one
problem . . . and you solve the next one . . . and then the next.
And if you solve enough problems, you get to come home.*

—Mark Watney in *The Martian*

MARK WATNEY IS THE MAIN CHARACTER in Andy Weir's
2011 novel *The Martian* that was adapted into a 2015 film

starring Matt Damon. Watney is a NASA astronaut who finds himself stranded at a space station on Mars when (spoiler alert) his crew accidentally leaves him for dead. Watney has to figure out how to survive on an uninhabitable planet for a couple of years until NASA can figure out a way to rescue him.

The Martian is fiction, but Mark Watney's problem-solving advice is rock solid social science.

When a ricochet event happens, our heads start spinning. Questions start pouring into our brains. *What does this mean? What's going to happen next? Why did this happen? How will this end? When will this end? Is this how I end? Why did I did do something so stupid? What am I supposed to do now? Where am I supposed to go? Who am I supposed to be? What will become of me?*

That's why the most adaptive people, to use Watney's term, "just begin." They do the math. Solve one problem, and then the next, and then the next.

Not long ago, researchers at Arizona State University found that when people get smacked with a big change—in this case, the death of a spouse—two simple activities distinguished the most resilient surviving spouses from the rest.

First, the resilient folks kept right on performing the tasks of their everyday work and life. Second, they remained actively connected with the people around them.

Stay engaged with work. Stay connected with people.

Those also happen to be two of the key ingredients in Chuck's recipe for successful adaptation, and the approach of the rest of the adaptive people in the Illinois Bell studies.

Instead of getting lost in lofty visions for a future that is wildly unpredictable and totally uncontrollable, and rather than getting hung up on old goals and dreams that no longer make sense. The Chucks of the world take one small step at a time, which is followed by another step . . . and another . . . and so on.

WHAT THE WHAT?

The big question is always *how?* How do you stay engaged with work when the old goals and plans of your work are suddenly rendered irrelevant thanks to a job transfer, a departmental reorganization, or a stifling new government regulation? How do you stay connected with people when the people you usually connect with are now a department, a city, or a world away?

Somehow we have to slow the spinning and grab hold of our thoughts again. We have to re-engage ourselves with the tangible tasks in front of us. A simple way to do that is by asking two questions.

1. What three things can I realistically accomplish in the next three months that will make the biggest impact on my team's success this year?

   2. What can I realistically accomplish in the
      next three days that will make the biggest
      impact on my team's success right now?

To keep your head pointed in the right direction, you can ask yourself these two questions that both conveniently start with *what*.

The three-month time frame in the first question lets your mind transcend the trivial and pursue the priorities.

A few years ago, Harvard researcher Teresa Amabile and her colleague Steven Kramer discovered that the number-one predictor of employee engagement is *not* whether a boss blankets you with warm fuzzies. (Nothing wrong with a little positive reinforcement, but tokens of appreciation alone won't get the job done.) Engagement also had nothing to do with the number of zeroes occupying the east side of your paycheck. More than anything else, people stay psychologically healthy and engaged when they feel like they are *making progress on work that truly matters.*

The three-day time frame in the second question lets you experience small doses of dopamine-pumping progress to keep you motivated even when the odds feel overwhelming. Isn't it amazing how checking a few things off your to-do list can magically make you breathe a little easier even when you're caught in an avalanche of personal setbacks or when you're just barely scratching the surface of an enormously difficult project at work?

When my wife is at work at the hospital dealing with a challenging patient in the critical care unit, she feels more focused and better able to make high-quality care decisions after she cleans the patient's room. She also feels better able to confidently challenge questionable care decisions made by doctors after they spend thirty seconds with a patient she's been taking care of for twelve hours. At home, no matter what is going on with our family, she always feels better after we clean the kitchen.

Neither of those things makes a huge impact on the "big picture." But they both restore her confidence about her ability to manage the situation. They bring her thoughts back into the realm of things she can control, instead of spinning aimlessly in the zero-gravity realm of stuff she has no control over.

These little bursts of progress correct the irrational belief that creeps into our minds and makes us think that we are helpless victims of our situation, instead of active shapers of the future.

Because both of the re-engagement questions are positioned in terms of your *team's* success rather than your own, you're forced to step outside of the solitary confinement cell that most of us (men especially) tend to put ourselves in whenever things start falling apart. These questions help you stay connected with the people around you. Their needs are now your needs. Engaging in *your* work necessitates staying engaged in *their* work.

PART 3

MAKE
MEANING

9

•

CHOOSE YOUR OWN
ADVENTURE

AT ANY MOMENT, YOUR LIFE CAN FALL into one of four quadrants based on how happy your life feels and how meaningful your life feels.

When your life feels happy but not meaningful, it's like being on a pleasure cruise. You're not curing cancer. You're not saving unfortunate souls from tyranny and oppression or helping the next generation create a brighter tomorrow.

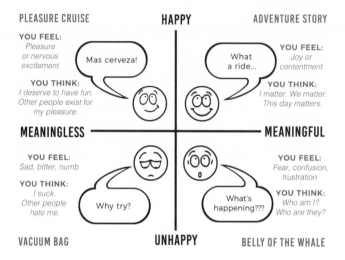

But it sure is fun! Although every now and then you wonder if there might be a little more to life than this, you also know something else: That waiter will be back any second. *Mas cerveza, por favor!*

When your life doesn't feel happy or meaningful, you're in a vacuum bag. It's dark and dusty and lonely in there. You can hear the world buzzing all around you as you tumble around from side to side completely at the whim of a herky-jerky invisible hand. But you don't really feel like you're a part of that world in any meaningful way. Sometimes you feel sad. Sometimes you feel bitter or angry. Other times you just don't feel anything at all.

I call it the vacuum bag because it sucks. But also because it refers to Viktor Frankl's "existential vacuum." That's the term Frankl assigned to that nagging sense of sedation and meaninglessness so many modern people experience.

The upside of a ricochet event is that it makes it really hard to have fun. By tearing off that veil of hedonism, the ricochet event puts us face to face with the gaping vacuum bag underneath. By finally exposing the vacuum, we're better able to fill it with something that makes our life meaningful.

When your life feels meaningful, but not happy, you're in the belly of the whale. You're not in your happy place. But you have this intuitive sense that the discomfort you feel has a purpose. You're being refined or transformed in some way, and maybe even for some purpose that still hasn't been revealed. Even though it's dark and scary and you're not sure when or where you'll get spit out, you have a feeling that something important is happening inside of you.

When life feels both happy and meaningful, you're the hero of an interesting and exciting adventure story. You can't be sure what you'll find on the winding path ahead. But you know it will involve mountains to scale, peaks to savor, grassy meadows to relax in, and dark caves to battle your way through. Even though you don't know what's going to happen, somehow you aren't afraid because the direction is clear and your steps are purposeful. You often feel pleasure. But it's more than that. It's pleasure *with* purpose and it's happiness *without* guilt. It's joy.

Before 2007, I had the spent the majority of my life bouncing back and forth between the pleasure cruise and the vacuum bag. Having so much fun sometimes that it should have beeen illegal (and *was* illegal on more than one occasion), and then at other times seeing the dean from *Animal House* staring back at me in the mirror, reminding me that "fat, drunk, and stupid is no way to go through life, son."

But then a series of ricochet events (baby, house, relocation, heart-attacked dad, etc.) sent me spiraling down into the depths of the vacuum bag deeper than ever before. Ricochet events have a unique way of cutting short your spring break in Acapulco and sending you packing on an alarmingly low-budget Ryanair flight in which the pilot asks the passengers to chip in for gas money before taking off (#ActuallyHappenedToMe).

But instead of simply climbing my way back aboard the pleasure cruise like usual, for some reason this time, I took a sharp right into the belly of the whale. Although I couldn't see it at the time through my heavy veil of self-pity, my parents noticed the subtle shift. I recall my dad making some joke about how he survived his heart attack only so he could live to see the day his arrogant, irresponsible, self-absorbed, Peter-Pan-syndrome-suffering son began transitioning into something more closely resembling a responsible adult who occasionally thinks about people other than himself. (I'm paraphrasing, of course. But not much. Love you too, Dad!)

In 2006, I was harvesting a bumper crop of happiness under a bright, beautiful sun. A year later, I was fighting with regurgitated chunks of plankton for a little elbowroom inside the big, dark belly of a whale.

DOES IT SMELL LIKE FISH IN HERE?

We have countless metaphors and myths from virtually every human culture—ancient and modern—that illustrate the dangers and the possible treasures of exploration. Probably the best-known tale of this ilk in Judeo-Christian culture is the story of a guy named Jonah. (Actually, the story of Luke Skywalker may have surpassed Jonah's in popularity by now.)

The gist of the story is that God asks Jonah to go help a bunch of people Jonah both despises and fears. So he responds to God with something along the lines of "Hmm . . . thanks for thinking of me. I'll get back to you. Don't call me, I'll call you."

Jonah then hops the first pleasure cruise he can find, headed for anywhere but there.

But the sea is angry that day, my friends. Presumably, because Jonah the yellow-bellied coward is on board. So the crew chucks him overboard. But instead of drowning, Jonah (luckily?) gets swallowed by a whale. Miraculously the whale swallowing doesn't kill Jonah. But while being digested, Jonah has a little me-time and begins thinking. *Who am I? Why am I here? Am I giving this whale irritable bowel syndrome?*

After a few days, the whale spits him out. After a few more days of scorching desert sun and a frustrating run-in with a misbehaving plant, Jonah finally decides to put on his big-boy pants and accept his fate. Turns out his enemies were more receptive to him than he had expected.

He's happy. They're happy. God's happy. Everyone's happy.

Virtually every culture has some variation of that story in which a ricochet event sends a main character to the top of a mountain, down the gullet of a big fish, into a dark cave, out into the desert, or to some other lonely and scary place. It happened to Shrek, Simba, Neo, Bilbo Baggins, Luke Skywalker, and thousands of other characters in countless movies, books, and TV shows.

Why? Because we can all relate. Sooner or later, we all end up serving a little time in the belly of the whale.

Maybe your whale belly is a departmental reorg. Maybe it's a divorce. Maybe it's relocation to a new city. Maybe it's an unexpected election result. Maybe it's the discovery of cancer in you or your mother or your husband or your daughter.

The bad news is that being in the belly of the whale doesn't feel like spending a week at an all-inclusive resort.

The good news is the belly of the whale can transform you into something stronger, braver, and wiser than you ever thought possible. Adaptive people don't "bounce back" from adversity, because they simply aren't the same person as they were before it happened. They allowed their time in the belly of the whale to transform them into something new and different.

Have you ever dreamed about living a more interesting, exciting, and meaningful life? The kind of life where you feel like you're truly alive, and other people tell you that you should write a book about?

Most people have that dream. And that life is available to all of us.

The rub is that this adventurous life isn't usually waiting for us on the nineteenth hole with a cold gin and tonic, or at the end of a rainbow. You can't get to it by floating on a drop of golden sun. You have to hop aboard the USS *Whale Belly* where the food is rotten, your cabin smells like fish, and it's impossible to find a clean bathroom.

The prize is available, but the price is higher than most people are willing to pay. We just have too much luggage to bring aboard and we can't bear the thought of leaving anything behind.

That's the hidden gift of ricochet events. They don't give you a choice before plummeting you into the nether regions of the vacuum bag or the belly of the whale. Ricochet events destroy the status quo, which is our default position.

But we do get to choose whether we spend this unhappy season in the vacuum bag or in the belly of the whale.

MEANING MATH

For most of my life, I made decisions based on the assumption that the quality of my life is directly related to the quality of the events that happen to me. Living the good life boiled down to what I call "happy math."

Happy math is a simple equation in which we try to make sure that the number of happy events in our life is greater than the number of sad events. So we work hard to make happy events happen—find good jobs, go to good schools, meet good friends, raise good kids, live in good neighborhoods, drive good cars, take good trips—anything that will increase the likelihood of happy events happening to us. On the other side of the equation, we try to prevent sad things from happening to us—avoid stressful jobs, steer clear of messy relationships, stay away from bad schools and bad neighborhoods, and generally avoid anything that might push the unhappy score higher than the happy score.

Because happiness was my primary metric, I tried to detach from difficulty, stress, and struggle—mine or somebody else's—whenever possible. Occasionally, I slipped up and accidentally helped someone for no reason. (I am only human, after all.) But overall I got pretty good at happy math. Sure I wasn't going to win a Nobel Peace Prize, but at least I'd be happy, right?

Wrong.

The problem with happy math is the undeniable fact that sometimes bad circumstances, terrible diseases, and nasty people will eventually find *you*. Sometimes good jobs are also stressful jobs. Sometimes good friends have difficult problems. Sometimes good kids have tough challenges.

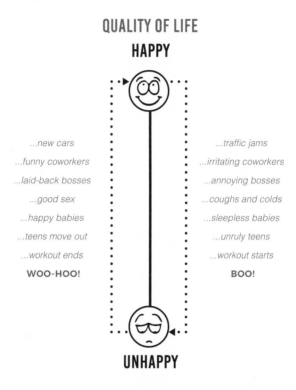

QUALITY OF LIFE
HAPPY

...new cars	...traffic jams
...funny coworkers	...irritating coworkers
...laid-back bosses	...annoying bosses
...good sex	...coughs and colds
...happy babies	...sleepless babies
...teens move out	...unruly teens
...workout ends	...workout starts
WOO-HOO!	**BOO!**

UNHAPPY

Despite our best efforts to craft a happy life, grumpy bosses, annoying coworkers, challenging kids, demanding partners, reckless drivers, deadly diseases, economic recessions, and pesky social-justice issues will always be there to inconvenience us. In some cases, half a lifetime of happy points can be washed away by a single tidal wave of unhappiness that no amount of preparation or planning could have prevented. What then?

When you strip it down to its bare essentials, the driving force behind happy math is not you. It's luck. That's the problem with happy math.

Now imagine if we started using a different scoreboard—one that depended on *you*, instead of on *luck*. I call this "meaning math." Instead of calculating happy events and unhappy events, you measure meaningful moments and meaningless moments.

In meaning math, you're the driver. When a senseless tragedy happens, you get to use it as an opportunity to score meaning points by summoning the courage to get through it for the sake of all the people who are waiting and watching to see what you'll do. For extra credit, you also help other people get through it instead of ruminating over the loss of your happy points.

When an upheaval at work happens, you look for ways to do something purposeful for yourself, your customers, your coworkers, or your company, instead of running away to your happy place in an effort to avoid losing happy points. When you have a chance to help someone, instead of seeing it as compromising your happy math, you see it as a surefire way to widen the gap between you and a life of sedation and nothingness.

Now, here's what you need to know about the four boxes:

Our circumstances will always be a key factor in determining whether we move up or down on the happy scale. No matter what you do—no matter how safe you try to play it—ricochet events will knock you off the happy pole. At which time, gravity will take over and pull you straight down.

When gravity takes over, where you end up will depend on where you were when you fell.

If you've chosen to pursue the pleasure cruise, your basement is the vacuum bag. That's where the gravity of change will drop you.

If you've chosen to live an adventure story, your basement isn't the vacuum bag. It's the belly of the whale.

Neither the vacuum bag nor the belly of the whale is pleasant. The difference is that the vacuum bag breeds only despair, while the belly of the whale inspires transformation. It makes us stronger and wiser. It makes us more adaptive. It prepares us to embrace the opportunities for adventure that are still ahead of us regardless of what is behind us.

10

•

THANK GOD IT'S TUESDAY

ONE SWELTERING TUESDAY AFTERNOON in the summer of 1776, a thin and lanky young man slumped down behind a desk in the tiny second-floor room of a red brick house on the outskirts of Philadelphia. The oppressive humidity made his thick, reddish-brown hair frizzier than usual as he swatted away houseflies buzzing through the window he'd propped open in a feeble attempt at colonial-era air conditioning. He sneered at the stable across the street—the source of both the flying parade of pests, as well as the unpleasant stench of horse dung.

Then suddenly, inspiration struck.

Something about recent events coupled with his skimming of the timeless treatises of John Locke and David Hume stirred his imagination. One thought spilled into the next. Ideas poured from his pen. Barely a day later, Thomas Jefferson had transformed a blank sheet of parchment into one of the most influential documents in Western civilization—a document that immortalized our relentless pursuit of happiness.

But here's the weird thing. When Thomas Jefferson felt inspired to promise us all that we had the inalienable right to pursue happiness, he was definitely *not* happy.

Already a sad and shy homebody by nature, he had just found out that his wife was gravely ill hundreds of miles away on his nearly bankrupt family farm. His second child in three years had died in infancy just months before. The ambitious junior statesman also firmly believed that all the important work was happening back at the Virginia statehouse while he was trapped up north trying to help manage a woefully underfunded and undermanned revolution that had so far produced nothing but a string of humiliating defeats.

And yet in spite of his misery, Jefferson was unquestionably inspired. How do we explain that?

Today the world's leading researcher in the scientific study of inspiration is Todd Thrash, who just so happens to be a professor of psychology at Thomas Jefferson's alma mater, the College of William & Mary in Virginia. A few years ago, Thrash stumbled onto something fascinating. He and his team rounded up a group of people and tracked how *inspired* they were, and how *happy* they were on each day of the week. They discovered that (drum roll, please) people are happier on Fridays than they are on Mondays. Shocker, I know.

But what about inspiration?

It turns out that even though people were most likely to feel *happy* on Fridays, they were least likely to feel *inspired* on Fridays. So what day of the week finds us most inspired? The same day of the week that Thomas Jefferson wrote the Declaration of Independence. The same day of the week that Mark Zuckerberg created Facebook. Possibly the most forgettable day of the week—little ol' Tuesday— is the crowned king of inspiration. And not just by a little bit. Inspiration was a full 79 percent more likely to occur on a Tuesday than on a Friday. Why?

Friday's the fun day. It's the day we cut loose our cares from the workweek and have a good time. It's a day devoted to pursuing happiness. I think that's a good thing.

But Tuesdays are different. On Tuesdays, we find ourselves in the thick of the workweek—immersed in the challenging, inconvenient, and stressful struggles of everyday life. It's a day for making things happen. That's also a good thing.

Many of the most inspired moments of our lives happen right there in the muck and mire of midweek stress when life is most challenging—when we're laboring to finish an important project at work; rallying a response to an unexpected dip in sales; begrudgingly accepting the coaching role for our kids' soccer teams; eating up our leisure time by lending a hand or a heart to people in need; or simply helping a friend lug a comically oversized couch up four flights of stairs.

In those moments we don't always harvest happiness, but we do till the soil for inspiration.

I wonder what would happen if we started looking forward to Tuesdays as much as we do Fridays? What if we pursued humanness (and all its attendant complications and mess) with as much vigor as we pursued happiness? Would we feel less sedated and more alive? Would stressful changes start looking more like invitations for adventure? Would we finally discover true happiness right where we least expect it—in the lives we're already living?

CONCLUSION

●

INTO THE BLUE AGAIN

And you may ask yourself, well
How did I get here?

—Talking Heads

AS I TYPE THESE WORDS, IT OCCURS TO ME that the March 2017 release date of *Ricochet* will come exactly ten years after Alison and I made that fateful cross-country move from San Diego to Minneapolis.

Today, I'm sitting in a Puerto Rican café where the house speakers are pumping out a steady stream of Fleetwood Mac and Natalie Imbruglia and The Cure and (what I can only assume is) Spanish pop music from the same period of the late twentieth century, all of which are accented by the sounds of Spanish-speaking voices volleying words back and forth over the sticky tables surrounding me. When I lift my eyes from the laptop screen and look out the window, I see the sun rising over the sprawling storefront of a Walmart Supercenter nestled in the foothills of the tropical mini mountains that blanket the island I've been calling home for the past five months. It's all strange and familiar at the same time. I can't help wondering which part of this scene Nick Tasler circa 2007 would view as more surreal—the geographic location, or the knowledge that a mile away sits *his* house with *his* minivan parked outside and *his* wife and *his* four kids inside.

Either way, I feel pretty certain that Nick 2007 did *not* see this coming. I'm also pretty sure the last ten years haven't unfolded how he would have scripted it. Bad things have happened that I wouldn't want to repeat. I've also made more dumb mistakes than I care to publicly admit.

And yet, many of the events from the past decade that Nick 2007 wouldn't have scripted are the exact same events Nick 2017 wouldn't trade. And some of the things Nick 2007 really, really wanted to happen—the wishes fulfilled and the goals met—turned out to be among the most disappointing and regrettable events of all.

I'm living proof of a truth that happiness researchers like Daniel Gilbert have shown pretty convincingly in recent years: human beings pretty much suck at predicting what will make them happy or sad in the distant future. You think you want that promotion until you finally get it and realize it wasn't the answer to your problems after all, or that the you who wanted that promotion long ago is simply a different person than the you who finally earned it. You think you want an easy, stress-free life until you find out that golfing or shopping every day is boring you to tears. On the flip side, you think you could never survive without this job, this marriage, this monthly income, this special person, or this way of life until the universe suddenly rips them from your fingers, and you find that you're somehow not only surviving, but on the verge of thriving, albeit in a very different way than you imagined.

The other night, Alison and I were watching the movie *Sully* about the doomed US Airways flight that eventually became the "Miracle on the Hudson." Alison commented how bizarre it is that on the one hand we all hope to never find ourselves in a harrowing situation like that, and yet on the other hand, we're all secretly jealous of the survivors who will forever have this amazing story to tell. That's the appeal of Batman, Harry Potter, and Snow White stories, and all those other classic tales of hard luck and tragedy that reveal secret identities and hidden strengths in their heroes. We're all instinctively drawn to these stories because we secretly want to find out what we're really capable of when a ricochet event hollows out our expectations and stretches us to the limits of who we can be.

I have no clue where I'll be ten years from today. And since I have no idea who you are, I have less than an inkling where you'll be ten years from today. But I feel pretty confident predicting that the next ten years for both of us will be an adventure filled with highs and lows, expectations met, and surprises encountered. And I'm absolutely certain that no matter what situations you find yourself in during the coming days or years, there will be freedom you can decide to find; progress you can decide to pursue; and meaning you can decide to make.

WORKS CONSULTED

WHAT HAPPENED WHEN MA GOT HER BELL RUNG

The stories of Andy and Chuck as well as the story of the impact of deregulation on Illinois Bell came from *Resilience at Work* by Salvatore R. Maddi and Deborah M. Khoshaba (AMACOM, 2005) and Maddi's book *Hardiness: Turning Stressful Circumstances into Resilient Growth* (Springer, 2013), as well as my personal email exchanges with Maddi.

The idea of the adaptive third was pieced together from a number of Roxane Cohen Silver's studies that I first discovered in the fascinating chapter she wrote in *The Psychology of Meaning,* edited by Keith D. Markman, Travis Proulx, and Matthew J. Lindberg (American Psychological Association, 2013.) Silver was gracious enough to clarify my musings and speculations in a string of thoughtful email replies. If you're interested in learning more about Silver's findings you might also consider checking out a chapter she wrote with Camille B. Wortman, "The Myths of Coping with Loss Revisited," in the 2001 edition of the *Handbook of Bereavement Research*, and another article she coauthored, "Searching for Meaning in Loss: Are Clinical Assumptions Correct" found in *Death Studies*, 24(6) (2000), pages 497–540.

THE KAFKA EFFECT

The details of Sarah Smith's story came from my personal interviews with her.

The British Columbia studies were published in a 2009 article "Connections from Kafka: Exposure to Schema Threats Improves Implicit Learning of an Artificial Grammar" in *Psychological Science.* The excerpt of the Franz Kafka's 1917 short story "A Country Doctor" was specifically manipulated by the researchers for purposes of their study. Their version was adapted from a collection of Kafka's short stories also called *A Country Doctor* (Kurt Wolff, 1919).

Charlotte L. Doyle wrote about seed incidents in "The Writer Tells: The Creative Process in the Writing of Literary Fiction," which can be found in *Creativity Research Journal*, 11:1 (1998), pages 29–37.

REVENGE OF THE PESSIMISTS

All mentions of Viktor Frankl's experience and ideas came from a combination of sources, including his books *Man's Search for Meaning* (1946) and *The Will to Meaning* (1969), as well as course material from the practitioner certification courses I took through the Viktor Frankl Institute of Logotherapy based in Abilene, Texas. You can track down the official chronology of his life on ViktorFrankl.org, which is listed as the official website of Viktor Frankl Institut in Vienna operated by his remaining family.

BE THE CHUCK YOU WANT TO SEE IN THE WORLD

The study about how acting extraverted makes you feel happier was conducted by psychologists William Fleeson, Adriane Malanos, and Noelle Achille and published in a 2002 issue of *Journal of Personality and Social Psychology* under the title "An Intraindividual Process Approach to the Relationship Between Extraversion and Positive Affect: Is Acting Extraverted as 'Good' as Being Extraverted?"

BACK TO THE FUTURE

The study "This Too Shall Pass: Temporal Distance and the Regulation of Emotional Distress" was conducted by Emma Bruehlman-Senecal and Ozlem Ayduk and published in 2015 in the *Journal of Personality and Social Psychology*.

Discussions of our perceived control over external situations have been ever-present in philosophy for millennia. Control is also one of the three Cs of hardiness or resilience (along with challenge and commitment) singled out by Salvatore Maddi. But it was probably the psychologist Julian Rotter who really formalized the study of perceived control back in the 1950s when he coined the term "locus of control."

THE MARTIAN PLAN

The study on spousal loss, "The Multidimensional Nature of Resilience to Spousal Loss" was conducted by Frank Infurna and Suniya Luthar, and published in 2016 in the *Journal of Personality and Social Psychology*.

Steven Kramer and Teresa Amabile's book *The Progress Principle: Using Small Wins to Ignite Joy, Engagement, and Creativity at Work* (Harvard Business Review Press, 2011) should be required reading for any manager interested in employee engagement.

THANK GOD IT'S TUESDAY

I pulled the details from the story of Thomas Jefferson's writing of the Declaration of Independence from *American Sphinx* by Joseph J. Ellis (Vintage Books, 1998).

If you want to learn more about Todd Thrash's work, I recommend starting with his 2014 paper "The

Psychology of Inspiration" written with Emil Moldovan, Victoria Oleynick, and Laura Maruskin and published in *Social and Personality Psychology Compass*, 8/9 (2014), pages 495–510.